New Media, New Politics?

From Satellite Television to the Internet in the Arab World

Jon B. Alterman

Policy Paper No. 48

THE WASHINGTON INSTITUTE FOR NEAR EAST POLICY

© 1998 by the Washington Institute for Near East Policy

Published in 1998 in the United States of America by the Washington Institute for Near East Policy, 1828 L Street NW, Suite 1050, Washington, DC 20036.

Library of Congress Cataloging-in-Publication Data

Alterman, Jon B., 1964–
    New media, new politics? : from satellite television to the internet in the Arab world / Jon B. Alterman.
        p.   cm. — (Policy paper ; no. 48)
    ISBN 0-944029-28-0 (pbk.)
        1. Communication, International—Arab countries. I. Title. II. Series: Policy papers (Washington Institute for Near East Policy) ; no. 48.
    P96.I52A733 1998
    302.2'0917'4927—dc21   98-44198
                                                                    CIP
Cover design by Debra Naylor, Naylor Design Inc.

About the Author

Jon B. Alterman is a program officer in the Research and Studies Program at the United States Institute of Peace. From 1997 to 1998, he was a Soref research fellow The Washington Institute for Near East Policy. Dr. Alterman received his doctorate in history from Harvard University, where he concentrated on the modern Middle East and U.S. foreign policy. He has worked as a legislative aide to Sen. Daniel P. Moynihan (D–N.Y.) covering foreign policy, defense, and intelligence, and in the U.S. Department of State's Bureau of Human Rights and Humanitarian Affairs covering Middle East issues. Dr. Alterman has lectured widely in the United States and abroad on historical and contemporary issues. He is the author of several journal articles and editor of *Sadat and His Legacy: Egypt and the World, 1977–1997* (Washington: The Washington Institute, 1998).

• • •

Contents

Acknowledgments

The idea for this paper came from a talk by Jihad al-Khazen at Harvard University in the spring of 1997. It has been a great pleasure to develop some of the ideas suggested in that talk with a variety of informants who have become good friends. I am particularly indebted to Mohamed Hakki, Shibley Telhami, and Hussein Amin. Each time I talk with them, I learn something new. I have also benefitted from discussions with the very talented group of Arab journalists in Washington and London who play an essential role in the processes described in this paper. For reasons of discretion I have not mentioned their names, but that in no way diminishes my appreciation for their help.

This paper is stronger than it otherwise would have been because of helpful readings, suggestions, and sometimes corrections by Omar Razzaz, Jon Anderson, Jane Gaffney, George Hishmeh, Eric Goldstein, and especially Ibrahim Karawan and Jihad Fakhreddine. A trip to London was made far more productive because of the assistance of Amr Abdel Samie. None of them should bear any responsibility for this text's deficiencies; I am fairly certain that each of them disagrees with at least one aspect of what I say here.

The research and writing of this project were carried out at The Washington Institute for Near East Policy, where I was a Soref research fellow during 1997–1998. I am grateful to the Institute's executive director, Robert Satloff, who saw the merit in this proposal from the start and supported my research throughout. Jonathan Lincoln provided helpful research assistance. Publications Director Monica Neal Hertzman and her assistant Elyse Aronson have always been a joy to work with and countless times have improved whatever grace my writing might have. My colleague Zoe Danon Gedal was a good friend in a difficult year, and I am thankful.

My wife, Katherine LaRiviere, has been a tremendous support to me through thick and thin. Words cannot begin to express my gratitude.

• • •

All translations from Arabic are the author's unless otherwise noted.

Preface

Information, the saying goes, is power. In America, the emergence of new technologies—from the internet to satellite and cable television—has produced an explosion of new sources of information that have given the average citizen access to vast resources of news, ideas, opinions, and data. This phenomenon has revolutionized the way people think about their government, culture, and society.

In the Arab world, where the heavy hand of government has long controlled television, radio, and the print media, the new technologies are also making their mark. From transnational newspapers and magazines published in Europe, to satellite television stations that broadcast political debates and call-in shows, to internet web pages and e-mail messages that travel anonymously or with encryption over international telephone lines, these new media are confounding old-fashioned censors and posing new challenges to regimes across the region. Although still in their infancy, with high cost and still limited access, these new media have, in just a few years, changed the Arab news, information, and entertainment markets beyond recognition.

In this study, Jon B. Alterman, a 1997–1998 Soref research fellow at The Washington Institute, explains the origins and implications of this media revolution. Through original research and numerous interviews, Dr. Alterman analyzes the changing relationship between Arab governments, their own local media (which they control), and the new media (which are largely beyond their reach). He also assesses financial and sociological aspects of the new media, ranging from the critical role of commercial advertising in the future success of new media to the ramifications of Arab reliance on Western—that is, American—movies and television shows for their viewing fare.

Although the overall picture he paints is positive—more access means more news means better informed citizens throughout the Middle East— Dr. Alterman does note some potentially negative trends in the new media phenomenon. These include the security challenges posed by terrorists exploiting the internet for their own nefarious ends and the political challenge of the emergence of what he calls a "new Arabism"—a media-driven transnational movement that is uniting Arabs across national boundaries, often in hostility to U.S. policies in the Middle East. For U.S. policymakers, he offers important advice: If satellites and web pages are going to be the battlefield for the hearts and minds of Arabs in the next century, then America needs to prepare a high-tech campaign of "information diplomacy" that is up to that challenge.

We are pleased to publish this important study as part of our ongoing effort to help the Washington policymaking community understand the challenges facing America in the Middle East in the coming decade and to prepare to meet them.

Mike Stein
President

Barbi Weinberg
Chairman

Executive Summary

In the last decade, a revolution has swept through the Arab world. While governments have, for the most part, remained stable, the ground on which they walk has shifted. Long accustomed to exercising control over what their publics knew and when they knew it, governments are finding that new technologies based on satellites and telecommunications have given rise to new kinds of regional media that are generally beyond those governments' direct control.

The first technological leap was the international Arabic newspaper, written with datelines throughout the Arab world, edited in London, and printed remotely in major world capitals using satellite communications. The international Arabic papers—most important among them *al-Sharq al-Awsat, al-Hayat,* and *al-Quds al-Arabi*—comprehensively and often authoritatively cover issues of importance to Arab readers, and they are available on the day of publication in most Arab capitals. The papers have also emerged as an important intellectual outlet for the region; the opinion pages of *al-Hayat* in particular are among the most varied and open fora for debate in the Arab world.

More recently, the 1990s have witnessed the rise of Arab satellite-broadcast television stations that challenge traditional state monopolies over television broadcasting. Despite multiple formats and multiple pricing schemes, few of the stations seem to have found a way to make a profit at this point. Viewers continue to flock to them, however, and satellite dishes continue to proliferate on balconies and rooftops throughout the Middle East. In addition to providing a diversion for viewers, the satellite television stations have played a significant role in breaking down censorship barriers in the region. They have encouraged open debates on previously taboo subjects like secularism and religion, provided fora for opposition political leaders from a number of countries, and given a voice to perspectives that were previously absent from the Arab media.

Most recently of all, in the last few years the internet has been making its way into the region. Although penetration remains quite low and the obstacles to its acceptance are high, the internet holds out the promise of allowing Arabs to dip into a vast sea of information that currently lies beyond their grasp.

Although it is too early to tell with certainty where the new technologies will lead, some broad outlines of changes appear clear. First, the efficacy of censorship will decline. With ever-growing amounts of information circulating at increasing speeds and decreasing costs, political systems predicated on restricting the information available to individuals will be sorely tested. The possible exception to this trend is Saudi Arabia. Because Saudi capitalists are so dominant in financing the regional media and are so closely tied to the Saudi state, and because Saudi consumers represent such an important market for regional advertisers, the kingdom is likely to retain significant influence over the regional print and broadcast media into the future. In terms of censoring internet transmissions, however, governments will find monitoring the technology ever more difficult. Although in its infancy, internet use will certainly increase, and with it the use of encryption software that can be used for good, such as by human rights organizations whose work from the region may have been previously prohibited, or for evil, such as by opposition groups planning terrorist attacks on a country.

Second, the Arab media are likely to shape the emergence of a new kind of Arab identity in the coming years. New technology allows Arabs across the region and around the world to read, see, and hear the same information at the same time to a degree that is unprecedented. This will have a unifying effect on Arabs within the Arab world, and it may also reintegrate Arabs living in North America and Europe into the Arab intellectual life.

Third, an exponentially expanding amount of information reaching Arab readers and viewers, combined with higher levels of education, will induce large numbers of Arabs to interpret information in new and more sophisticated ways. Governments will have to change how they interact with their citizenry, as on the one hand governments will have lost their monopoly over information, and on the other, they will have an increasingly difficult time convincing their publics to support ill-considered or ill-justified policies.

The manner in which these changes manifest themselves will be influenced by the future shape of the Arab media. If such media prove commercially viable, change will occur sooner, because market-driven content will respond to the interests of varied populations of individuals rather than those of governments. Should the new media require long-term subsidies, they will reflect the interests of those who can finance them: either states themselves, or wealthy individuals tied closely to states, especially Saudi Arabia.

Even so, the difficulty of containing information will increase rather than decline, and the long-term trends appear likely under any circumstances.

For the U.S. government, which often enjoys more support among Arab governments than among Arab populations, a more open media environment is a mixed blessing. On the one hand, the United States supports human rights in general and freedom of expression in particular, and the new technologies are likely to prove a boon to free expression. On the other hand, public opinion in much of the Arab world has been turning against the United States in recent years, and the new technologies can facilitate stirring up anti-U.S. sentiments. Governments may be harder pressed to support U.S. policy lines in the future, absent public support.

The imperative is for Washington to engage the new Arab media. American officials should seek out opportunities with Arab journalists to make a case for U.S. policy. American officials should appear on camera and explain the U.S. position to a possibly hostile audience. Whereas some in U.S. foreign policy and defense circles object to explaining their positions even to the American public, the new technologies and the changes they are causing in the Arab world and beyond make such efforts necessary. The price of failing to do so may prove high indeed.

Chapter 1

Introduction

W hen Americans and Europeans traveled to the Middle East in the nineteenth century, time after time they were struck by the image of an "unchanging East." Gazing upon peasants, crops, and draft animals, they felt transported back to Biblical times. Ignorant of the upheavals of the intervening two millennia and of the rapid changes then underway in the Middle East, they projected placidity and stability onto a situation in which there was little of either.

A similar misjudgment occurs in current assessments of the Arab world. Popular accounts of the region that see it as either a stagnant backwater or, worse, a collection of unstable and regressive societies hurtling back to the fourteenth century, miss much of what has been happening in the region and many of the opportunities that the next decade will present.

In fact, the Arab world may be poised on the brink of fundamental change. "May be poised," not because the elements of that change are not yet present, but because the conditions in which those elements will combine and interact remain uncertain. The changes underway may radically alter the relationships between states and citizens, those between states, and those between the region and the rest of the world.

Part of this impending possibility of change is generational. The so-called "new middle class" that came to prominence in the Arab world in the post-mandate period is now mostly a spent force. States that, in the 1960s, were led by dynamic 35-year-olds find themselves with the same leaders, now aging, tired, and bereft of new ideas. Militaries that came to power on the promise of good government and eliminating the excesses of the *ancièn régime* are now widely accused of the same kinds of mismanagement, corruption, and cronyism that so ignited their passions in the revolutions that they made. Standing in the wings is a new generation: one more cosmopolitan, more comfortable with private enterprise, and less dedicated to the existence of a powerful state than its predecessors.[1] Although it is by no means certain that the members of this new generation will soon constitute the political leadership in the Middle East, their ascendance in political and economic life is unmistakable.

Another crucial factor in the transformation, and the subject of the following study, is the changing nature of the news media and information technology. As has often been remarked, the political borders in the Middle East are artificial creations, drawn by French and British cartographers to reflect European national interests. Allegiances in the pre-mandate Middle East were mainly to cities of origin, and with the exception of unusual cases like Egypt, the concept of "nationhood" or "national identity" was absent.[2] Among the first tools enlisted in creating a national identity was the national press. Improvements in printing allowed daily newspapers to flourish, which in turn nurtured the development of national literatures. In part influenced by the actions of mandatory authorities, ideas about censorship arose at the same time that these national literatures were created. Midway through the twentieth century and beyond, censorship became an increasingly dominant part of literary and intellectual life in many Arab countries. Although repressive, censorship—combined with state-sponsored media and culture—fostered a heightened sense of national identity in country after country.

The creation earlier in the century of national media structures in Egypt, Syria, and other countries led to a heightened sense of nationhood, and the eclectic national media of Lebanon symbolized Lebanese diversity; yet, the rise in the last decade or so of regional Arab media outlets—and, indeed, of a regional media market—challenges such developments. International Arabic newspapers and satellite television broadcasts, as well as the riches of the internet, bring to Arabs throughout the Middle East—and throughout the world—real-time, mostly uncensored, and authoritative news about their countries and their region. As the significance of geographical distance decreases worldwide with the developments of the Information Age, these new Arab media outlets promote the creation of a regional elite where national elites had heretofore been unchallenged.

Although the nation-state is not dead in the Arab world or elsewhere, it is certainly in a state of flux. Nonstate actors like multinational corporations and religious organizations have taken on increasing prominence in the Arab world, and vast public-sector industries have been on the retreat. The rise of international Arab media outlets (particularly ones that are less print-based and thus harder to regulate than before) is a further challenge to state dominance, as they are largely beyond the control of any individual state.[3] In a world in which information is a valuable commodity, the increasing openness of borders to information exchange empowers individuals and organizations with information and undermines states that have lost their traditional role as a gatekeeper for commodity exchanges.

States still retain the preponderance of power almost everywhere, and that seems unlikely to change in the near term. But the role of the state is bound to change, and the increasing flow of information across borders will play a major role in that change. In the Arab world, which has generally experienced a high degree of state control over information, the rise of new transnational Arab media will play a major role in that transformation. Although the outcome remains unclear, the status quo appears more tenuous now than it has been at any time in the last half century.

As influential as the new regional Arab media are, however, they still reach only a small percentage of the Arab population in the Middle East. Only about 10 percent to 15 percent of all Arabs have regular access to satellite television, a smaller percentage reads the international Arabic press, and a smaller number still is proficient with the internet. Cost is certainly a barrier for many, as is illiteracy.[4] With all of the exuberance about changes brought on by new technology, one should nevertheless consider the following data: According to a study by the Center for Strategic Studies at the University of Jordan, 95.6 percent of Jordanian households have televisions, but only 12.6 percent have satellite dishes. The study also found that Jordanian domestic programming attracts 57 percent of the viewing audience, compared to 17.5 percent for the satellite broadcasts.[5]

That said, those with access to regional Arab media are among the leaders of their societies—often the wealthiest, most educated, and most politically engaged. They are the leaders and opinion-shapers, and their thoughts and actions have an influence far beyond their immediate circle. The study that follows does not evaluate the importance of Arab public opinion,[6] nor is it a study of likely changes in Arab politics and governance over the next decade. It does not explicitly examine the Arab–Israeli conflict, although the Arab media will certainly affect it. Rather, this study is an exploration of the emergence of the new Arab media, a phenomenon that, despite having gone largely unnoticed in the United States, is poised to shape the region in the near future.

In this period of flux, the regional Arab media constitute both a force for change and a force influenced by change. The emergence of vibrant regional media will affect government actions in the region, just as government actions will affect the media. Although some factors influencing the region's transformation are external —especially those involving technological advances—for the most part the changes of the next decade will be products of the interactions of governments, news organizations, marketing interests, and the 250 million Arabs who are at the same time citizens, viewers, and consumers.

The direction in which all this will go is far from clear. More than reaching conclusions, this paper seeks to outline the factors likely to influence social and political change in the Arab world in the next decade. They bear attention and study.

Notes

1   Israeli prime minister Binyamin Netanyahu, who replaced the "old generation" of Israeli leadership in 1996, fits the characteristics of this ascendant class as well.

2   The notion of "Arabism" gained some currency in the early years of the twentieth century, mostly as a response to Ottoman (non-Arab) rule. More particularistic loyalties predating national identity included those to tribe, clan, and family (both one's own and that of the local nobility).

3   Saudi Arabia is a possible exception to the phenomenon of the media challenging the state, as Saudi nationals own such a large stake of the international print and satellite television operations, and Saudi consumers are the most attractive targets for regional advertisers.

4   The barrier of illiteracy exists even for broacasters. The formal Arabic used in television and radio reporting is close to the written language and is difficult for illiterate native speakers to understand. Even when colloquial Arabic is spoken, the differences between dialects are more easily overcome by literate Arabs than by illiterate ones. Whereas illiteracy is declining in the Arab world, it still hovers above 50 percent in many countries.

5   Dr. Fahd al-Fanak, "Watchword," *al-Arab* (in Arabic), July 10, 1998, p. 3. I am grateful to Prof. Ibrahim Karawan for bringing this article to my attention.

6   For a study on the importance of Arab public opinion, see David Pollock, *'The Arab Street': Public Opinion in the Arab World* (Washington: The Washington Institute for Near East Policy, 1992).

Chapter 2

Print Media

The history of the Arabic-language press stretches back to the early nineteenth century. Western soldiers and missionaries brought the first presses with movable type to the Middle East, and local governments used the new technology both to publish official information and to pass on news and entertainment. By the dawn of the twentieth century, newspapers had been published in Cairo, Baghdad, Algiers, Tunis, Damascus, Sana'a, and Khartoum.[1]

Even at this early date, an expatriate Arab press existed in Europe. During the last decades of the nineteenth century, Yaqub Sanu' published the satirical *Abu Nazara Zarqa'* in France and shipped it to Egypt. Later, Islamic reformist scholars Jamal al-Din al-Afghani and Muhammad Abduh published their religious journal *al-Urwa wa-al-Wuthqa* in Paris.

Expatriate publishing remained a relatively small part of Arab intellectual life, however. Domestic journalism spread throughout the region in the twentieth century as literacy became more common, colonial bureaucracies grew, and mass politics began to evolve. By the end of World War II, many Arab capitals boasted a number of newspapers occupying varying points on the political spectrum. Like European newspapers, these Arabic papers generally had explicit party ties and constituted an important part of the public political debate.

The Egyptian revolution of 1952 ushered in a new kind of Arab government—independent and nationalistic—and with it came a new kind of press. As single-party political systems replaced the fledgling multi-party systems of the colonial era, governments turned to the press to exhort the public to support the new rulers. Many governments closed the party presses and replaced them with government organs that reflected official viewpoints. In 1954, for example, the Egyptian regime shut down *al-Misri,* the newspaper of the leading Wafd party. Soon after, *al-Misri*'s presses were turning out *al-Gumhuriya*, a new regime mouthpiece whose editor was the voluble propagandist—and later Egyptian president—Anwar Sadat. The nationalization of Egyptian publishing in 1961 merely made formal what had been true informally for years: that the written word was to be employed in the service of the state. Throughout the region—in Syria, Iraq, Libya, and South Yemen, among others—governments took over the ownership of the press. Arab media analyst William Rugh's characterization of these newspapers as the "mobilization press" is apt, as the purpose of the press was to rally support for essentially authoritarian governments.

The mobilization press was not always a purely domestic operation. Egypt was particularly active in promoting its views throughout the region in the late 1950s and into the 1960s, not only through the semi-official Egyptian daily *al-Ahram*, but also through vigorous radio broadcasting. *Sawt al-Arab* (The Voice of the Arabs) combined the attraction of Egyptian singing stars like Abdel Halim Hafez and Umm Kalthoum with pro-regime news reports to reach a broad audience during this period. Readers in all the Arab countries closely followed the columns of Mohamed Hassanein Heikal, editor in chief of *al-Ahram* and widely known to be a confidant of President Gamal Abdel Nasser. In Egypt's bid for the leadership of the Arab world, the country instituted a bold media strategy that was an essential component of the political program.

Government ownership of the press was not the rule in every Arab country. In some, governments worked out understandings with local newspapers, allowing them to operate in private hands as long as they were generally supportive of government policies. Rugh calls these publications, many of which still exist, the "loyalist press," as they are "consistently loyal to and supportive of the regime in power despite the fact that they are privately owned."[2]

At the time of the October 1973 Arab–Israeli war, a familiar governmental model prevailed in the region. Arab governments carefully controlled their elections, and few Arab countries had anything resembling a free press. This is not to say that public opinion did not exist, or that it was irrelevant. Governments mixed coercion with co-optation, carefully monitoring public opinion so as to understand what might lay beyond the bounds of popular acceptance. In addition, many governments allowed a kind of loyal opposition to emerge, permitting a diversity of views within understood boundaries. Doing so allowed new ideas to gestate and kept the intelligentsia in line without threatening the government's ultimate grip on power. The media—initially the printed press, later radio, and still later television—played an important role in this equation by both disseminating government viewpoints and providing a forum for carefully modulated criticism and commentary on government policies.

There were important exceptions to the general pattern of having the media serve the state. For much of this century, Lebanon maintained a tradition of an eclectic and relatively free press. With its unusual mix of ethnic and religious groups denying any one group majority status, Lebanon developed a tolerance for diversity of opinion unmatched anywhere else in the Arab world.[3] Beginning under the French mandate and continuing well beyond, Lebanon saw the emergence of a large number of newspapers and magazines representing all facets of Lebanese life and opinion.

The freedom of the Lebanese press led factions from all over the Arab world to support financially—overtly or covertly—Lebanese publications sympathetic to their viewpoints. Beirut therefore became something of an *entrepôt* of political parties, religious groups, and foreign intelligence organizations seeking to use one publication or another as a mouthpiece for their views. In this way, the city became the Middle East's intellectual crossroads, a place where Nasserists, royalists, Shi'is, Maronites, and others debated openly.

The Lebanese civil war forced much of Beirut's intellectual community into exile. No longer safe when warlords ruled the streets, Beirut's writers and editors sought refuge abroad, first in Cyprus, then mostly in France, but also to a significant degree in the United Kingdom. There, many reconstituted the publications they had built in Beirut, and they also built new ones.

Europe in the late 1970s also spawned a new kind of Arab newspaper. Beginning in 1978, a company called Saudi Research and Marketing (discussed below) began producing *al-Sharq al-Awsat* in London, and it used satellite technology to beam the paper's contents to printing plants in Saudi Arabia.[4] The paper's editor was Jihad al-Khazen, a veteran of the English-language press scene in Beirut and former editor of the Beirut *Daily Star*. Because the new newspaper was headquartered in London, it had ready access to Western news sources. Further, because it was written and edited in London, it was not subject to the same kinds of government restrictions it would have been were it produced in Saudi Arabia.

Al-Sharq al-Awsat was the harbinger of a new kind of Arabic press. Followed by a reborn *al-Hayat* (a Beirut paper that had stopped publishing during the war, was resurrected in 1988, and was given new life in 1990 with an infusion of cash from Saudi prince Khalid bin Sultan) and *al-Quds al-Arabi*, London became the locus for a lively Arab press scene. In addition to the newspapers, the London-based publishing houses also began turning out an impressive array of glossy full-color magazines: *al-Majalla, al-Wasat*, and others. All of these publications thrived on the freedom of their European base, and all were available to varying degrees throughout the Arab world, although occasional issues would not make it past local censors in one country or another in a given week.

The London-based publications shared something in addition to their heavily Lebanese cast of writers and editors: To a large degree, they relied (and continue to rely) on subsidies from the Persian Gulf. In fact, London's dominance over Paris in fostering the development of a vibrant press testifies to the relative importance of money in getting these enterprises operating. On the whole, the Lebanese who represented the majority of expatriate Arab editors and writers in exile would have been more comfortable in Paris, as the second language of Lebanon is not English but French. Gulf Arabs, however, were on the whole more comfortable in English, and it was mostly to London rather than Paris that they traveled when the oil boom of the 1970s brought new prosperity to the Middle East. The journalists followed the money. Over the last quarter-century, London has emerged as one of the world's great Arab capitals, with banks, restaurants, shops, and a vibrant and open press previously unknown in the Arab world itself.

SAUDI RESEARCH AND MARKETING

Saudi brothers Hisham and Muhammad Ali Hafiz are the public face of Saudi Research and Marketing (SRM). The company is controlled by Saudi prince Ahmed bin Salman, whose father, Prince Salman bin Abel Aziz, provided much of the capital for the company. Former head of Saudi intelligence Kamal Adham holds a large private stake and plays a behind-the-scenes role. Scions of an old Saudi press family, the Ali Hafiz brothers began publishing the English-language *Arab News* in Jeddah in 1974. Four years later, the company transferred the editor of *Arab News*, Jihad al-Khazen, to London, where he launched a dramatically new kind of paper, *al-Sharq al-Awsat*, edited in the United Kingdom and distributed in the Middle East. Conceived as a paper to be printed remotely using new satellite printing technology, it is today printed simultaneously in Jeddah, Riyadh, Dhahran, Kuwait, Casablanca, Cairo, Beirut, Marseilles, Frankfurt, London, and New York. It is the only international paper printed in Saudi Arabia, which enables it to be on the newsstands early in the morning—not an insignificant competitive advantage.

The daily paper, the outside pages of which are dyed a distinctive green, is professionally well-respected, although it is closely identified with the Saudi government. Stories are legion in Arab press circles about Saudi "sensitivities" that make their way into editorial decisions at the paper, especially those that involve the royal family or any form of *lèse-majesté* more generally. *Al-Sharq al-Awsat* is not merely a mouthpiece for the Saudi regime, however. Its pages host a relatively wide variety of views, and it is followed as one of the best indicators of developments in the Saudi kingdom. Its circulation is estimated at some 242,000, with a claimed readership of ten times that number.[5]

The sister publication of *al-Sharq al-Awsat*, the weekly magazine *al-Majalla,* is similarly solid. An impressively produced publication, one of its strengths is its wide variety of columns from regular contributors. In a single issue's pages, Abderrahman al-Rashed may be critical of Islamist movements, Fahmy Huweidy may view them favorably, and Hassan Hanafi may view them in a positive, somewhat leftist light. Whereas *al-Majalla*'s columnists do not share uniform views, they are generally well within the Arab mainstream. *Al-Majalla*'s news coverage is similar to an American publication like *Time* or *Newsweek*, blending hard political news, social issues, and consumer-oriented stories. Often engaging, it is rarely shocking.

Al-Majalla is part of a stable of eighteen different SRM publications. The company produces three women's magazines (led by the highest-circulation Arabic magazine, *Sayidaty,* which sells some 140,000 copies per issue), the men's lifestyle magazine *Arrajoll*, the children's magazine *Basim*, an Arabic *TV Guide* (directed at the regional satellite television market), and specialized newspapers for religious news and sports news. SRM's genius has been to understand how to turn Arabic publishing into a money-making operation. Its approach has been to integrate the publishing operation vertically. SRM owns not only a publishing company, but associated advertising and distribution companies as well. Because it is able to capture money that would otherwise go to other firms, SRM is in the black— the only company of its kind that has been able to achieve this feat.

The readership for SRM's publications is primarily Saudi Arabian. *Al-Majalla*, for instance, has an audited circulation of just under 100,000,[6] and some 85 percent of its readers are reportedly Saudi. An estimated two-thirds of *al-Sharq al-Awsat*'s readers are Saudi, and the paper's status as the "prestige" Saudi paper, along with its excellent distribution system and presence on newsstands first thing in the morning, ensures healthy advertising sales. Circulation is boosted by Saudi government subscriptions; for example, Saudi students in the United States receive free subscriptions to *al-Majalla*, which constitute a large portion of the publication's U.S. circulation.

JON B. ALTERMAN

AL-HAYAT PUBLISHING

Whereas SRM has found a way to make a profit through Arabic publications, most Arabs regard *al-Hayat* as the premiere Arab paper. Although commercially it runs a deficit every year (estimates are generally in the $10-million range), *al-Hayat* has emerged as the leading forum for opinion makers in the Arab world to debate various points of view. The paper claims a daily circulation in the neighborhood of 168,000 copies, and it is printed at eight sites throughout the world (nine, when Marseilles is added in the summer months).

Al-Hayat is the London-based reincarnation of the Beirut paper of the same name. Founded by Kamel Mrowe in 1946, the paper survived its founder's assassination in 1966 (reputedly for his stand against Nasserism) but it could not withstand the ravages of the Lebanese civil war. The paper shut its doors in 1976 and emerged twelve years later in London. Until he stepped down in the spring of 1998, the editor of *al-Hayat* in its present incarnation was Jihad al-Khazen—the same person who had launched *Arab News* and *al-Sharq al-Awsat* in the 1970s. Khazen's idea seems to have been not only to provide a prestigious forum for diverse points of view, but also to begin to stretch the limits of censorship throughout the region. Whether he and his financial backers were motivated by idealism, journalistic zeal, or a desire to reconstruct the press freedom of Lebanon throughout the Arab world is unclear, but *al-Hayat* has played a major role in breaking down barriers to censorship in the region, sometimes at a cost to itself.

If Khazen is the brains behind *al-Hayat*'s success, the money behind it belongs to Prince Khalid bin Sultan, son of the Saudi defense minister and a multimillionaire (perhaps billionaire) in his own right. Although Prince Khalid's motivations are known only to himself, knowledgeable observers suggest that he views *al-Hayat* as a vehicle that both gives him official entré in the Arab world and provides him with an occasional forum for his political views. Whatever its publisher's motivations, *al-Hayat*'s success is judged not on its turning a profit but rather on its importance as an opinion-shaper in the region. To this degree, the paper has succeeded remarkably well. It is no accident that Fouad Ajami's most recent book on Arab intellectual life is based heavily on articles, columns, and poems that appeared in *al-Hayat* over the last ten years.[7]

To a greater degree than almost any other Arab news outlet, the prospect of censorship appears to weigh heavy in the minds of *al-Hayat*'s editors and writers. In the battle over censorship issues, each country has its particular sensitivities. Tunisian censors, for example, are wary about stories concerning Islamic politics in the region, and Jordanian censors closely watch stories involving Arab relations with Israel and criticisms of King Hussein's "rush" toward peace. In recent years, Egyptian authorities have banned any publication that airs the views of Omar Abdel Rahman, the blind Egyptian cleric currently serving time in a U.S. prison for his incitement of terrorism while in the United States. As a paper distributed throughout the Arab world, *al Hayat* must balance the interests of its broad readership with the ability to distribute in any individual country.

The consequences of censorship for a newspaper like *al-Hayat* vary. Saudi Arabia is *al-Hayat*'s biggest market, and also the location of most of the consumers its advertisers target. Being banned in Saudi Arabia costs *al-Hayat* something on the order of $50,000 a day. Being banned in Sudan, however, may actually save the newspaper money, as the cover price does not come close to the cost of distributing the paper there.

Overall, *al-Hayat*'s editors believe that occasional banning in any given country helps the credibility of the paper, as it demonstrates the newspaper's independence from governmental interference. In practice, however, *al-Hayat*—like all newspapers—cannot alienate the governments that are its sources, and Khazen maintains a close personal contact with many rulers in the region.

Despite its high-level ties, the sometimes outspoken paper has made some serious enemies through the years. In January 1997, *al-Hayat* itself made headlines when its offices in New York City, Washington, London, and Riyadh were targeted by a letter-bombing campaign. The bombs reportedly arrived in envelopes bearing Egyptian postmarks, but no culprit has ever been publicly identified, nor has a motive for the bombings been established.

Al-Hayat's daily print run is about 200,000 copies. About half are printed in Bahrain, mostly for the Saudi market.[8] According to unaudited circulation figures supplied by *al-Hayat,* daily sales in Saudi Arabia run about 80,000 copies. *Al-Hayat* sells an additional 18,000 copies in Western Europe (printed in London and Frankfurt); 10,000 in Lebanon; 7,500 in Morocco; 7,000 in the United States (printed in New York); and 3,500 in Egypt.[9] Other countries account for fewer daily sales. Day-old copies are shipped from Saudi Arabia to Sudan, where the absence of other news sources ensures that there is still a demand for day-old papers.

In addition to the newspaper, al-Hayat Publishing Company produces a glossy magazine called *al-Wasat*. Launched in 1992, the magazine offers coverage of Arab and international events. Each issue begins with a series of 250-word briefs from the magazine's correspondents around the world, and continues with a long newsmaker interview, news and analysis of regional events and individual countries, several business features, some coverage of fashion, features on Western and Arab celebrities, automobile reviews, sports reports, social pages, book reviews, and a few puzzles. A column signed by Khazen—often involving Western issues as much as Middle East ones—concludes every issue. *Al-Wasat* is not the success that *al-Hayat* is: It is not nearly as well known in the region, and its advertising sales remain weak. Its circulation, estimated at about 76,000, significantly trails that of its competitor, *al-Majalla*. In addition, its straight-news format does not lend itself to being the same forum for a wide variety of viewpoints that is the hallmark of *al-Hayat*. Nevertheless, its comprehensive and balanced coverage of political news makes it one of the leading magazines of its kind in the region.

AL-QUDS AL-ARABI

Trailing far behind in resources is *al-Quds al-Arabi,* a daily paper published out of London under the leadership of a dynamic Palestinian editor, Abdel Bari Atwan. In no way part of a publishing empire, *al-Quds al-Arabi* publishes with a handful of reporters out of somewhat threadbare offices in the London suburb of Hammersmith. Nevertheless, the newspaper has emerged as an important voice in expatriate Arab circles, and to a lesser extent in the Arab world itself. The newspaper's strength is its reporting—generally based on anonymous sources—of decisions and events in the Arab world. The newspaper also features an important innovation: a page every day with complete translations from the Israeli press.

Editorially, *al-Quds al-Arabi* is reliably the most strident of the important Arabic papers. When U.S.–Arab tensions heat up, it is *al-Quds al-Arabi* that is most likely to publish a scathing attack on the American position and the least likely to publish a defense or explanation of U.S. policy. In addition, *al-Quds al-Arabi*'s news coverage focuses more than any of the other papers on Arab–Israeli issues. Finally, *al-Quds al-Arabi* is the only one of the "big three" that does not rely on Saudi Arabian sources for funding. As a consequence, the paper enjoys a freedom to talk about Gulf politics and events that its competitor publications do not.

One of the most distinguishing characteristics of *al-Quds al-Arabi* is its dearth of advertising. With circulation mostly limited to New York, London, and Frankfurt, the paper may have one or two paid advertisements per issue. Atwan is believed to have attracted financial support from a variety of sources since the paper began nine years ago, including the Palestine Liberation Organization, Iraq, and Sudan. Knowledgeable sources suggest that the paper currently may be subsidized by the government of Qatar, which would square with Atwan's high-profile criticism of Saudi financial control of international Arab media outlets, as well as with the paper's support of an Arab nationalist line.

SMALLER PUBLICATIONS

Rounding out the stable of subsidized daily Arab papers published out of London and distributed worldwide are *al-Arab*, published by former Libyan information minister Ahmed Salhin al-Houni, and *Azzaman*, published by Saad al-Bazzaz, an Iraqi expatriate who maintains ties to the regime in Baghdad. Both papers fairly closely reflect the national views of their sponsors, and both resemble the Arab domestic press of the 1950s and 1960s far more than the publications described above. In that regard, their news and editorial focus is somewhat narrowly restricted to issues of Arab unity and opposition to Israeli and U.S. policy. They rail against the unfairness of purported U.S. and Israeli control of international institutions, they are blind to domestic news, and they cover neither intellectual developments nor human interest stories. In addition, their coverage of news is restricted rather narrowly to the actions of the top one or two officials in any given country, ignoring the descriptions of internal factions and decision-making processes that play such a large role in the Western press and in the other expatriate Arab newspapers. The circulation of these papers is unclear. Just as difficult to define is their audience, which quite clearly is not the Westernized elites who constitute such an important readership for the other papers.

In addition to these papers, a large number of newsletters and small-circulation magazines exist in the Arab world. Partly a product of the last decade's explosion of desktop publishing, many of these publications have a niche market and low overheads. Some are Islamist in character, some are based on political opposition, and some expose scandal (or, reportedly, extort payments in exchange for *not* exposing misdeeds). Many rely on a mix of some or all of these. Whereas their reach is generally not international, they represent an important part of the growing mix of journalistic products available to readers in the region.

Finally, the internet has been playing an increasing role in the distribution of news, if not necessarily printed newspapers. At this writing, more than thirty Arabic newspapers are available online, including all of those described above. The effect of online information will be discussed more extensively in chapter 4, but it is important to note that the internet allows editors and writers throughout the Arab world to read each others' work on a real-time basis. This development helps to promote (yet does not by itself create) the emergence of a more unified journalistic "voice" throughout the region, notwithstanding the dispersion of writers and editors across national borders throughout the region and the world.

SUMMARY

Arab newspapers have gone through several cycles of change this century, as many became party organs and were later enlisted in the service of the state. In the last decade, technology has allowed a new kind of Arab paper to emerge—one that is international in both its creation and its audience. Whereas regional Arabic newspapers and magazines reach only the elites in most countries, they constitute an important avenue for regional dialogue, and they play a significant role expanding the sphere of public debate.

NOTES

1   William Rugh, *The Arab Press: News Media and Political Process in the Arab World*, 2nd rev. ed. (Syracuse, N.Y.: Syracuse University Press, 1987), p. 18.

2   Ibid, p. 71.

3   Lebanese diversity is in many ways analogous to the religious and ethnic diversity that prevailed in British North America, and which gave rise to a system of religious pluralism that characterizes the United States to this day.

4   The Gannett Corporation relied on similar technology when it launched *USA Today* as a national U.S. newspaper in the early 1980s. The technology has since become common.

5   *Middle East and Africa Market and Mediafact* (London: Saatchi and Saatchi Advertising Worldwide, 1997), p. 85. All print circulation figures from the region should be considered with some caution, as a common form of subsidy is to purchase a large number of copies that are not read and sometimes not even delivered. Circulation figures do give a rough guide, however.

6   At the time of this writing, Audit Bureau of Circulations data is available at http://chianti.ipl.co.uk/abc/enquiry2.html.

7   Fouad Ajami, *The Dream Palace of the Arabs: A Generation's Odyssey* (New York: Pantheon, 1998).

8   Fewer copies of *al-Hayat* are printed in Bahrain in the summer months, when Saudis travel abroad to escape the summer heat. During that time, *al-Hayat* prints in Marseilles, France.

9   Circulation figures supplied by an *al-Hayat* editor in London, March 1998. According to a circulation sheet provided by the company's advertising agency, in 1997, circulation was 83,000 in Saudi Arabia; 7,500 in the United Arab Emirates; 2,700 in Bahrain; 2,300 in Oman; 4,600 in Kuwait; 2,300 in Qatar; 7,500 in Yemen; 8,250 in Egypt; 9,500 in Lebanon; 1,800 in Morocco; 5,600 in "other Middle East"; 15,700 in Europe; 7,800 in the United States; and 9,700 in "other Western World," for a total daily circulation of 168,250.

Chapter 3

Satellite Broadcasting

S atellite television is an innovation that has burst onto the Arab scene only in the last decade. Indeed, television itself is no more than a few decades old in most Arab countries. Egypt did not begin television broadcasts until the early 1960s, and Yemen began only in the mid-1970s. From its inception, Arab television was closely controlled by state broadcasting authorities. Its news programs were heavily scripted and almost invariably led with extensive coverage of the activities of the head of state.[1] Entertainment programs trod delicately on social (let alone political) issues, and the consequence was a diverting yet not particularly exciting extension of the state information apparatus into the homes of the populace. Television programming was the product of government bureaucrats, and it often showed.

Today, satellite dishes are sprouting up all over the Arab world. Although estimating their exact numbers is a perilous science, close observers of the satellite scene estimate that some two-thirds of the population in the Persian Gulf has access to satellite television, about 20 percent of Palestinians, and perhaps 10 percent of Egyptians and Syrians.[2] Officials of the most widely viewed channel, the Middle East Broadcast Centre (MBC), optimistically estimate their audience "at minimum, 100 million to 120 million viewers."[3] Whereas such estimates may be fanciful, the audience for Arab satellite television is nonetheless substantial, even in authoritarian countries like Iraq and Syria. Assessing the exact audience for satellite television is nearly impossible. This author's own estimates, based on marketing information, as well as on discussions with broadcasters and scholars of the Arab media scene, suggest that somewhere between 10 percent and 15 percent of Arabs in the Middle East regularly watch satellite broadcasts.

Three developments in the Arab world led to the rise of satellite television in the 1990s. The first was the multilateral response to Saddam Husayn's invasion of Kuwait. To a great extent, Operation Desert Storm and its preceding events in 1990–1991 made for wonderful television programming. Pentagon public relations experts understood the importance of public opinion on the conduct of the war, and although the war was not a "made-for-TV movie," it supplied highly impressive images for news broadcasts. In addition, the Pentagon's "spin operation" ensured that there was a constant outpouring of carefully controlled information from the allied side. The result was a feeling of immediacy and a steady stream of information for television viewers.

Cable News Network's intensive coverage of the war, including its impressive production values, attractive announcers, and array of experts, made many Arabs perceive their own domestic broadcasts to be drab and lifeless affairs.[4] As attractive as CNN was to watch, it was not available in most Arab homes during the war. The requisite antennas were large and expensive, and distribution was oriented to commercial establishments like hotels rather than to the home market. In addition, CNN's English-language broadcasting proved a barrier to easy comprehension by many Arabs. Nevertheless, the presence of CNN helped to forge a market for a new kind of Arabic broadcasting.

Another crucial development for the sudden emergence of Arab satellite television was the launch of a new generation of satellites. Arabsat, a consortium comprising the members of the League of Arab States, launched its first communications satellite in 1985. Using the technology of the era, reception of television broadcasts from the first Arabsat satellites required huge roof-based antennas that cost many thousands of dollars. There is now far more capacity to broadcast to the region than ever before, and the requisite antennas are shrinking and becoming more affordable, owing in part to technological advances, the launch of several new and more powerful satellites in the 1990s, and the popularity of a new band (Ku) set aside specifically for direct-to-home broadcasting. Today's antennas may be as small as 50 centimeters (less than 20 inches) across, and they can be positioned easily on a balcony or concealed (if need be) with little difficulty. As satellites become more powerful and occupy lower orbits in the sky, there will likely be a continued increase in broadcasting capacity as well as a continuing diminution in the size and expense of satellite dishes.

The third important development was the emergence of a substantial class of Arab professionals who had studied and sometimes worked in the West before returning to their countries of origin. Those from the Gulf countries especially benefitted from sharp increases in levels of education, literacy, and prosperity following the oil boom of the 1970s. They are also products of the jet age, when a trip to Paris or London is a voyage of merely a few hours. Some 200,000 Saudis have studied in the United States since the early 1960s, and tens of thousands of others have studied in Europe.[5] Other Saudis have lived in Western countries for extended periods for other reasons. And Saudi Arabia is not alone; in country after country around the Gulf and throughout the Arab world, a dramatic increase in foreign travel occurred in the 1970s and 1980s, coinciding with an increase in educational opportunities, literacy, and wealth.[6]

This growing numbers of Arabs who lived overseas were more consumer-oriented than were their parents, and their wealth gave them many options for consumption. Back home, many missed the entertainment and information outlets to which they had grown accustomed during their time in the West. This group—and their children—have formed much of the core market for fee-based satellite television services like Orbit and ART (Arab Radio and Television). Satellite broadcasting offered these viewers an avenue back to the culture they experienced abroad, and an avenue for advertisers of luxury goods and brand-name commodities to reach their target audience. Satellite television does this partly by rebroadcasting Western television programs and films, and also by adapting the methods of objective reporting and open political debate toward issues of interest to Arab viewers. In the words of promotional material for the Orbit network, it is "geared towards an audience of educated, well-traveled, and affluent professionals for whom culture, entertainment, and up-to-date information have become a necessity."[7]

The costs of producing satellite television broadcasts are difficult to ascertain. None of the stations file annual financial reports, and in interviews with representatives of the satellite broadcasting companies it became clear that they regard their cost structures as privileged business information. Satellite broadcasting clearly requires serious money. The annual fee for renting the use of a satellite transponder is estimated to be some $4 million per channel. The cost of producing and buying programming is then added to that and clearly runs in the tens of millions of dollars per year for each of the stations involved. Hundreds of thousands of additional dollars are invested in computers for digital graphics, remote-controlled cameras, sets and lighting, and other aspects that contribute to a "fresh" on-air look for the Arab networks.[8] MBC and the Arab News Network (ANN) produce their news in one of the most expensive cities in the world, London, increasing costs still further for the regional broadcasters.

Satellite broadcasters have two sources for income: advertising revenue and subscription fees. With regard to the first, advertising is less well-developed in the Arab world than in other developing regions like Southeast Asia and Latin America. Indeed, annual advertising expenditures in the entire Arab world barely exceed those of Israel alone.[9] Still, advertising in the Arab world is growing, and regional broadcasters are able to land a larger and larger share of annual spending. According to a recent study, total spending on regional satellite television advertising is currently $90 million, with some 70 percent of that split between MBC, LBC (the Lebanese Broadcasting Corporation), and Future Television.[10]

The general consensus is that few if any of the regional broadcasters could break even on the basis of advertising revenue. The one thought to be closest, LBC is estimated to derive about half of its $45 million annual revenue from its terrestrial (i.e., local) broadcast and half from satellite operations.[11] Whereas MBC representatives categorically refused to discuss their revenues or expenses, they pointed to an article that estimated their annual advertising revenue at $27 million.[12] Even so, the station is widely perceived to be hemorrhaging money. Management shake-ups have been routine, and whispers abound that the station's fortunes may fall with the ailing health of Saudi Arabia's King Fahd, who has been a significant booster for years. The new phenomenon in the field, Qatar's al-Jazeera station, has not released revenue figures, but two things seem certain: Advertising fees are discounted heavily over published rates, but revenues will rise with the station's obvious popularity among regional viewers.

Another possible source of revenue for regional broadcasters is subscriptions. Orbit was the regional pioneer in sending encrypted signals over the airwaves and then requiring the purchase of a proprietary decoder box and "smart card" to ensure payment of monthly fees and pay-per-view charges. ART was a later entry to the field, as were global players Star TV (sold as an add-on to Orbit in the Middle East) and Showtime; meanwhile, LBC reportedly plans a premium pay channel in addition to its free-to-air offerings.[13]

Monthly fees for pay channels are steep—$50 a month and up, in many cases—with additional channels available for additional monthly fees. The pricing puts pay-TV services out of the reach of most Arab viewers, especially those from moderate-income countries like Egypt and Jordan. The viewers it does draw, however, are those who would be among the most attractive to advertisers: the wealthiest and most consumer-oriented.

Whereas satellite television in the United States and Western Europe has developed almost entirely along the fee-for-service route, indications are that the Middle East may be a holdout for free-to-air broadcasting, albeit alongside pay television. This is partly because much of the regional audience cannot afford expenditures of hundreds of dollars a year for programming, as well as because individuals and governments are more willing than those in the West to sustain losses on their broadcasting operations in the region. The key to all of this is the development of the advertising market and Western-style consumption patterns, as they will determine the amount of revenue available to stations and, by extension, whether losses will have to be sustained indefinitely, and at what magnitude.

MIDDLE EAST BROADCASTING CENTRE

The oldest and most established station, as mentioned above, is the Saudi-owned MBC. It is the standard against which all other stations are judged, and it is certainly one of the most widely viewed channels in the region. MBC's flagship product is its news programming, which comes on five times a day. The station's editors gather their news from many of the same sources used by CNN and other international television news operations: newspapers, wire services (in Arabic and English), satellite news gathering operations (like World Television News, AP Television, and others), and a network of correspondents throughout the Middle East and the rest of the world.[14] A senior editor in MBC's news operation said he considers CNN to be his chief competition, and he delights in scooping his better-established and better-funded rival, especially on matters of interest to his Arab audience.[15]

It is their knowledge of the audience and the sources that MBC editors and reporters believe gives them the edge over their Western competitors when covering news of the Arab world. With a news staff that represents most of the countries of the region (albeit with something of a predominance of Lebanese, Egyptians, and Palestinians), the MBC newsroom is a melting pot of ideas and backgrounds that produces something resembling a "unified Arab view." In addition, their knowledge of the region allows MBC reporters and editors to read between the lines of wire service reports and newspaper copy to gain a more complete understanding of a news story than may be apparent at first glance. Whereas other Arab news operations have similar dynamics, MBC was the pioneer in this field.

MBC was the leader in revolutionizing Arab news coverage. The first Arab television company to open a Jerusalem bureau, MBC's coverage of Palestinian affairs has been based on interviews and on-the-ground observations rather than on polemics and third-hand reports. Perhaps more important, MBC has led the charge to cover news that previously had been ignored in Arab media. From the coverage of an attempted coup in Algeria in January 1992 to its intensive coverage of the Israeli assassination attempt on Hamas operative Khalid Mesh'al in Amman in 1997, MBC's news coverage has shined light on events that may make governments in the region squirm, but about which regional audiences are hungry to know.

MBC is also a regional leader in presenting documentaries prepared for a global audience to the Arab world. The station caused a stir in March 1997 by airing a seven-part documentary on Operation Desert Storm that stood at odds with many governments' official versions of events. The series, produced by a company owned by two editors from the Saudi Research and Marketing conglomerate,[16] featured interviews with Arabs from the coalition forces, Iraqis, Israelis, and Western officials. Never before in the Arab world had such contrasting views been presented on a topic of such political sensitivity. Indeed, the Kuwaiti foreign minister stalked out of his interview for the series when it became apparent that he would be subject to more critical questioning than that to which he had been accustomed in his previous dealings with the media.[17] The series also aired previously secret footage of regional leaders squabbling at an Arab League meeting in Cairo, which tarred the image of Arab solidarity that the leaders had been seeking to present. One viewer from the United Arab Emirates told a reporter, "Me and my friends just had to get together every night to watch . . . Then we'd have the most intense political debates we've had since the war."[18]

More recently, MBC aired a five-part documentary from the same production company entitled "The Fifty-Year War . . . Israel and the Arabs." The British Broadcasting Corporation originally aired the series in the spring of 1998; a version was broadcast on Israel's Channel 2 in the autumn of 1998 and will air on public television stations in the United States in January 1999. The documentary has caused significant discomfort for government officials in the region. On April 26, 1998, the Jordanian Royal Court officially denied the program's assertion that, following a meeting of King Hussein, Syrian president Hafiz al-Asad, and Egyptian president Anwar Sadat just days before the 1973 War broke out, the king tipped off Israeli prime minister Golda Meir that war might be imminent. Many viewed the fact that the Jordanian government had to deny the allegation rather than merely censor it as a sign of how much satellite television has changed modes of operating in the region.

In addition to its news programming, MBC also features talk shows, music, films, and serials. It was a partner with the Voice of America in a pioneering program called "Dialogue with the West," which brought together experts and officials from the Middle East and the United States for eighty episodes. Begun in 1995, the language of the broadcast was Arabic, with simultaneous translation in the studio for non-Arabic-speaking guests. The program was an initial hit but ran into problems as American guests perceived its objectivity to be declining over time. Amidst the beginnings of a congressional uproar in November 1997, the show was quietly dropped.

MBC's regional audience is impossible to estimate accurately. Informed sources suggest that a highly rated MBC show may attract an audience of 500,000 or so in Saudi Arabia. Yet, Saudis are more likely to have satellite dishes than other Arabs, and they are more likely to watch television as well.[19] MBC's news shows are also available on the services of several domestic broadcasters, which swells the audience in other countries. A maximum audience estimate of around 2 million for a highly viewed show seems to be in the right neighborhood then, although the numbers may be higher or lower.

Ownership of MBC is controlled by Shaykh Walid al-Ibrahim, a young Saudi investor whose holdings also include United Press International. Al-Ibrahim's sister is married to King Fahd, and familial ties have reportedly played a role in gaining financing and support for the shaykh's media ventures, which include wiring the Kingdom of Saudi Arabia for microwave television reception. His personal wealth is estimated as high as $9 billion,[20] suggesting that he can afford to run deficits at MBC for some time before running out of cash.

Some industry observers whisper that, despite its history of innovations, MBC is today a troubled company. For one, the station is perceived to be the personal project of King Fahd, who is now ailing. A joke making the rounds a few years ago had MBC standing for "*My* Broadcasting Company," and stories abound of King Fahd calling the station and asking them to show one program or another as his mood dictated. MBC's somewhat daring programming—although less daring than its competitors, as will be discussed below—certainly benefitted from its royal protector, and it is unclear whether MBC can remain as free from interference by conservative Saudi forces under a new regime. MBC's programming is thought to be rather staid compared to that of its competitors, and the loss of its chief patron could make it even more so and therefore less attractive to segments of the viewing audience.

A second perceived problem with MBC has to do with its management. In the station's short life, management shake-ups have occurred with regularity. Within the station, rumors of layoffs, new initiatives, and further changes are rife. In a fast-paced, competitive global environment, the top-down decision-making and secrecy that appears to characterize MBC's management style may hamper the station's ability to respond quickly to emerging challenges.

Ultimately, observers say, MBC has to come to some conclusion as to its identity as a company. Continuous subsidies have allowed it to buy top-of-the-line equipment and to maintain a high-quality staff of Arabs and Britons, and it has emerged as the standard for Arab news broadcasts. But caution in programming has led some to see the station's products as stale, and a commitment to remain in London (to maintain a greater degree of independence) has raised the costs of production far above those of most of its competitors. If MBC is to be a successful business venture (which its management insists is its goal), industry analysts suggest it will be necessary either to take steps to bring its costs in line with its competitors or to derive sufficient competitive advantage from its London base to cover the increased costs of doing business there.

AL-JAZEERA

The hot story in Arab satellite broadcasting is the Qatari station, al-Jazeera. A relative newcomer to the regional scene, al-Jazeera went on the air from Doha only in November 1996. Al-Jazeera is an all-news channel, with a difference: it intentionally seeks to be provocative in a region in which news reporting has often been the private fiefdom of government information ministries, and in which dissent has been tightly controlled. Al-Jazeera revels in presenting unusual views and political debates. Its two flagship programs, *al-Ittijah al-Mu'akas* (The Opposite Direction) and *al-Ray al-Akhar* (The Other Opinion) are debate programs, and heated ones at that. Taking their cue from American programs like the *McLaughlin Group* and *Crossfire*, al-Jazeera's debates often present diametrically opposed perspectives on issues that matter to Arab viewers: religion and politics, relations with Israel, regional unity, and others. In addition, the station is closely tied to the Qatari government,[21] and the government's low-grade rivalry with Saudi Arabia allows the station to report and comment on Saudi news with a freedom unparalleled in the region.

The station has been subject to assaults from conservative Saudi sources. Calling al-Jazeera's broadcasts "another kind of pornography," commentator Muhammad bin Salman al-Ahmad complained in the Riyadh daily newspaper *al-Jazira*:

> On this station, Arab and Muslim speakers meeting on Arab land and using Arabic are subjected to vicious and ferocious attacks against their values, principles and beliefs . . . Some of the programs transmitted on this

satellite channel talk about the sacred divinity, whether it exists or does not exist, may God forgive us; they talk about the holy Koran, whether it was created or revealed; they talk about the Islamic Shari'a, especially about the penalties for theft and adultery, and whether these are appropriate to the spirit of the new age, describing them sometimes as abhorrent and criminal. How does a simple Muslim in the Arab world or in the Gulf region feel . . . when he listens to and watches a debate going on about the values, beliefs, and principles he had taken for granted?[22]

The answer from viewers is often, "Fascinated." Although some see al-Jazeera and its meteoric rise as something that will just as soon burn itself out, many in the region and in the Arab diaspora regard it as a breath of fresh air and gripping television.

The vast bulk of al-Jazeera's talent comes from Arabs who have lived in the West. The host of *al-Ittijah al-Mu'akas,* Faisal al-Qasim, received his Ph.D. from the University of Hull in England and worked for the BBC's radio and television Arabic services from 1988 to 1996. He told an Arabic-language magazine in the spring of 1998, perhaps hyperbolically, "Not twenty percent of the freedom of expression available to me on the Jazeera channel was available to me on the BBC. Room for freedom on the Jazeera channel is immense, and it is one of the reasons for the success of the channel."[23] The format of his program closely mirrors Western examples: Two guests with opposing views debate—sometimes harshly—a question of the day. Some of this is informational, but as al-Qasim admits, it contains an element of entertainment in it as well.

The debates often produce lively fireworks. In a widely seen show, Jordan's then–deputy prime minister, Abdel Raouf al-Rawabdeh, debated Jordanian Islamist opposition leader Layth Shbaylat. Shbaylat, who has been imprisoned numerous times for rhetoric that bordered on incitement to violence (and whom King Hussein personally freed several times), angrily attacked the Jordanian government throughout the show, and the minister responded in kind. After its broadcast on al-Jazeera, Shbaylat challenged the Jordanian government to rebroadcast the debate so all Jordanians could see it. The government did, but rather than build support for Shbaylat, the result seems to have been mere titillation. To the audiences that watched the show with their satellite dishes, and later with their roof antennas, and later still on videotapes that passed from hand to hand to hand, the scene was nothing short of remarkable.

Al-Jazeera is a startling new experiment for state-run broadcasting in the Arab world. It trumpets its bold independence and provides a forum for criticisms that otherwise have difficulty finding an outlet, especially critiques of the Saudi Arabian and Bahraini governments. The effect is to make Qatar—a state with only 150,000 citizens and a working-age population that is 83 percent foreign[24]—a serious player on the regional stage. Qatari power as a consequence of al-Jazeera emanates from two sources. First, were the government of Qatar to try to influence news coverage, the widely watched station could help to shape public opinion in the region. Broadcasters assert that the station enjoys complete independence,[25] but most viewers expect that a state-owned and -run station will show some deference to government concerns and agendas. Indeed, domestic Qatari issues such as the power struggle between the current emir and his father, whom he displaced, do not find an outlet on al-Jazeera, nor do critiques of Qatari foreign policy. Second, al-Jazeera's encouragement of openness and full debate has a powerful influence on other societies in the region. By featuring guests and subjects whose political views would otherwise be banned in various countries in the region, al-Jazeera's programs undermine censorship in individual states and expand the bounds of freedom throughout the region. Whether and how this advances Qatari goals (and what those goals might be) is unclear, but it certainly gives Qatar greater regional influence than it might otherwise have.

LEBANESE BROADCASTING CORPORATION (LBC)

If al-Jazeera indicates that news can be entertainment, LBC indicates that entertainment can be news. Eschewing the searching debates affecting the Arab soul that typify al-Jazeera's coverage, LBC's formula is to provide music, variety, and a bit of scandal in the search for an audience. Rather than settle for middle-aged men in suits, the presenters on LBC are often attractive young women in revealing clothing. The station's approach is perhaps best typified by the program *al-Layl Layltak* (The Night is Yours), whose description reads, "A programme that receives a celebrity not to be interviewed as usual, but to be surrounded by 4 girls who ask him unusual, funny, and embarrassing questions."[26] In a similar vein, what is perhaps the channel's best-known program is a morning exercise show entitled *Ma Illak Illaa Hayfa* (Hayfa Is the Only One for You), which features attractive women dancing to modern music in leotards. A joke making the rounds for months is that the station's proper name is not the acronym LBC but rather the Arabic word *ilbissi*, which is the second-person feminine imperative form of the verb "to get dressed."

Although LBC's appeal to prurient interests to build its audience is unusual in the region, it is clearly not unique, given that *Baywatch* is the world's most widely syndicated program. LBC's more sexually provocative programs exist alongside serious news and Western-oriented entertainment. In addition to its own news and entertainment programming, LBC rebroadcasts CNN International and *ABC News* daily, and it also shows vintage American programs (the *Cosby Show*, *Get Smart*, and *Hawaii Five-O*) and Hollywood films. Rather than exist as a Middle Eastern version of *The Playboy Channel,* LBC has emerged as a sort of amalgam of Arab and Western culture (a role with which many in Lebanese society are generally comfortable), and perhaps a harbinger of what Arab television would look like as a purely commercial venture and not one financed (and often subsidized) by conservative Gulf Arabs concerned with providing quality "family" entertainment.

LBC's decision to provide "light" entertainment with sexual overtones has made it a market leader, especially in terms of profitability. In conversation after conversation, regional broadcasting authorities and industry officials agreed that LBC is probably the only station in the region to turn any sort of profit. There is agreement, however, on another point: What may be racy on Arab television might appear mundane on some European channels. Were more explicit Western channels widely available, LBC might not be willing or able to compete in providing titillating entertainment, and the formula could collapse. The spread of digital broadcasting technology—and its attendant ability to fit more and more broadcasting channels on a single satellite—increases the possibility that a racier alternative to LBC may emerge, either from within or from outside the region. The station's franchise, then, will depend on its understanding of the regional market and its ability to blend Arab and Western culture in a way that is appealing to regional viewers.

ARAB NEWS NETWORK (ANN)

The newest entry on the regional satellite broadcasting scene is the Arab News Network. Begun in the summer of 1997, the station is operated by the 27-year-old nephew of Syrian president Hafiz al-Asad, Sawmar al-Asad, and hopes to establish itself as a regional news channel akin to CNN. According to an Arabic weekly magazine, *al-Watan al-Arabi,* the younger Asad said ANN's goal would be to "address social, economic, and political issues" in the Arab world and not shy away from discussing "social ills" in individual countries.[27] The younger Asad told the *Financial Times* in 1998 that ANN exists "to tell the Arab people that their voices will be heard."[28]

Sawmar al-Asad's proclaimed populism, as well as the open rift between his father and the president, has led some to view ANN as a political

weapon rather than an orthodox news outlet. When the Syrian president re-
lieved his brother Rifaat of his position as Syrian vice president in the spring
of 1998, at least two Arabic publications suggested that Rifaat's media activities (and those of his son) were a primary cause of the dismissal.[29] All
discussions of the tensions that ANN has caused between different wings of
the Asad family mention ANN's decision to air videotaped footage of Saudi
Arabia's Crown Prince Abdullah attending a party in Syria hosted by Rifaat
in the summer of 1997 (the two are related by marriage). The Syrian government apparently interpreted the move as an attempt by Rifaat to demonstrate
that he has Saudi backing and therefore is a suitable successor to his es-
tranged brother should the latter die or become incapacitated.

The Saudi angle of ANN has been a persistent rumor in its first year of
operation. ANN's financing is less clearly understood than that of any of
the Arab television stations, as there is no "visible" investor. Sources close
to Sawmar al-Asad told a London-based Arabic newspaper that the money
for the station came from Rifaat (who has the millions to lavish on such an
operation), but persistent rumors circulate in London and elsewhere that
ANN's money comes from Saudis close to Crown Prince Abdullah.[30] Some
close observers of the region suggest privately that, in fact, the former is
true, but that the station encourages rumors of Saudi support so as to gain
a sort of imprimatur and to encourage outside investment from Saudis and
others.

Amidst this intrigue, the station's news operations have begun to attract notice. The professional London-based staff has, by most accounts,
begun turning out well-informed and accurate news broadcasts. Feuds with
the Syrian government seem to be waning since ANN's Syrian correspondent was released from prison and ANN has taken a generally less-critical
tone toward the Syrian regime.

ANN has evolved into something of an enigma on the regional broadcasting scene. Suspected of having the clearest political agenda and the
muddiest backing of all the regional broadcasters, the station's evolution
will be one of the more interesting developments of the next few years.
Some assert that all of the speculation about ANN is misplaced, and that it
is merely a business venture that will soon be sold off to the highest bidder
seeking a turnkey operation that can be used as a prestigious franchise.

ORBIT

All of the above channels are free-to-air operators; that is, they beam their
signals down from satellites and can be viewed for free by anyone who

installs an appropriate antenna. As such, they rely purely on advertising for their revenues. In the last five years, stations in the Middle East have begun raising revenues in a different way: by encoding their transmissions and selling proprietary decoder boxes to subscribers. The result is that subscribers pay a monthly fee for enhanced programming, much in the same way that cable and satellite subscribers in the United States pay monthly fees for the additional channels they receive.

Orbit was the pioneer in extending fee-based satellite broadcasting to the Arab world, and the journey has not been without its bumps along the way. When broadcasting began in May 1994, the first obstacles were the exorbitant pricing of the decoder boxes (reportedly $10,000) and the huge satellite antennas (ten feet across) necessary to receive programming. Initial demand was slack, but it has picked up significantly as the cost and size of equipment has decreased. Orbit now claims 180,000 "viewing points," although many of those points consist of hotel rooms that may or may not be occupied by guests tuning into Orbit broadcasts.[31]

Orbit's programming choices are perhaps the most explicitly Western of the Arab channels. Featuring locally adapted versions of ESPN and the Disney Channel, a "Super Movies Channel" featuring Western films, an "America Plus Channel" with American situation comedies, and other American offerings, Orbit allows Middle Eastern viewers who can afford the subscription fee the ability to tap into current American popular culture.

In addition to its English-language offerings, Orbit broadcasts two of its own Arabic channels. The first is dedicated to Arabic films (and Western films dubbed into Arabic). The second features a variety of Arabic entertainment programming. Its most important program is a daily interview show, *Ala al-Hawa'* (On the Air), with Egyptian broadcasting veteran Emad Adeeb. In the last several years Adeeb has interviewed many of the leaders of the Arab world, live and on camera. Although the program is not as contentious as the programming on al-Jazeera, the high-level leaders who appear on the program are subjected to much closer scrutiny than they might be from their own domestic media. *Ala al-Hawa'* features a call-in segment, which allows regional viewers to question and sometimes challenge their leaders in a way that is unique in the Arab world.

Orbit's experimentation with regional news programming started off a bit rocky, however. When it first went on the air, Orbit contracted with the BBC Arabic service to produce news for the station. Tensions flared when the BBC aired stories that Saudis found objectionable, including coverage of the London-based Saudi dissident Muhammad al-Mas'ari, and a report on the *Panorama* show that explored the issue of capital punishment in the

kingdom. Orbit's American chief executive officer, Alexander Zilo, released a statement in April 1996 that called the show "a sneering and racist
attack on Islamic law and culture," and canceled the BBC agreement.[32]

On the entertainment side, Orbit is a partner in providing regional access to Star TV, which supplies programming from the American network
NBC; cable stations CNBC, the History Channel, and the Computer Channel; and other sources. Star Select, as the service is known, is part of Rupert
Murdoch's Asian satellite television empire. Business is likely smoothed
by the fact that Zilo came to Orbit from Murdoch's Star TV operation. At
this point, Star TV seems to have concluded that it is better to partner with
an established Arab firm to reach the Arab market rather than compete
head-on.

Fees for Orbit remain steep. A promotion running in the United Arab
Emirates in June 1998 made all the channels available for one month, and
a selection of English-language channels available for an additional three
months, for a fee of $345. After the initial period, a subscription to the
English package costs about $59 per month. Purchased à la carte, Orbit's
two main channels combined are $18 per month, the Disney Channel an
additional $15, Orbit–ESPN Sports another $18, and the Star Select package $26. All told, typical annual subscriptions to Orbit appear to run about
$900 or more, at least for home viewers.[33] In a region where per capita
incomes in many countries are significantly less than twice that, Orbit for-
goes a significant part of the viewer market, albeit the portion that is less
attractive to most regional advertisers.

Of greater import, perhaps, is the perception of some that Orbit's services are too Western-oriented for many Arab viewers' tastes. Orbit's "bouquet" of offerings is heavily oriented toward unmediated Western
programming, from situation comedies to a channel that rebroadcasts the
major American network news shows. Although a collection of expatriate
Western workers and well-traveled Gulf Arabs may represent a sufficient
market to allow Orbit to break even, it is likely to prove an obstacle to
Orbit achieving a dominant role in regional political and social debates. Its
Arabic news and variety channel may hold sway with a rarified group of
intellectuals and businessmen, but it seems impossible to achieve the audience penetration of channels like al-Jazeera or MBC.

It is not clear, however, that Orbit wants to play a leading regional
role. Orbit may represent the triumph of the profit motive in regional programming, a daring experiment to demonstrate that a regional broadcaster
can make money without resorting to the titillation of LBC. It is possible
that Orbit's victory will be in demonstrating that, for those concerned with

profits, satellite broadcasters in the Middle East—like those in the United States—will have to rely on subscriber revenues rather than distributing their signals for free.

Orbit is owned by the Mawarid Group, a multi-billion dollar Saudi business conglomerate controlled by Prince Khalid bin Abdallah, which sunk an estimated $2.3 billion into the station's start-up. The station's headquarters are in Italy, although subscription operations are carried out in Cyprus and many of the shows are produced in the Arab world.

ARAB RADIO AND TELEVISION (ART)

The other influential regional player in subscription-based satellite television is Arab Radio and Television. A former investor in MBC, Salah Kamel, began the company in 1994 when he sold his 37.5 percent stake in MBC for a reported $60 million.[34] Another major investor is Prince al-Walid bin Talal, the Saudi billionaire whose holdings include large chunks of EuroDisney, Citicorp, Apple Computer, and a host of other investments. ART began as a free-to-air multi-channel service but changed to a modified subscription-based system in 1997. ART currently maintains one free-to-air "promotional" channel, but overall the company relies on subscription fees for the bulk of its revenues.

In contrast to its competition, ART's regional broadcasts do not put a heavy emphasis on news. In addition to its promotional channel, ART broadcasts five channels (variety, kids, sports, movies, and music) that feature mostly Arabic-language programming. Eschewing the Western programming that is a staple of Orbit, its closest competitor, ART seeks to be a premium entertainment channel for Arab audiences. Indeed, Kamel told a reporter in 1995 that he started ART to "combat" Western satellite programming. "There is a Western media campaign to undermine our Arab culture and traditions," he said, adding, "I don't allow anything on ART that I wouldn't want my children to watch."[35]

ART's greatest problem is finding programming that will distinguish it from its competitors. There is a finite amount of Arabic programming available, and exclusive rights are hard to obtain. ART has invested heavily in the new Media Production City being erected outside of Cairo; that involvement may prove crucial to producing new shows that can both fill ART's considerable air time and convince the viewing audience that ART is worth the premium charged.

When Kamel founded ART, its offices were in Italy. Within a few years, however, they began to migrate to Cairo, which put them closer to their audiences and also to production facilities. Costs in Cairo are also a fraction of the costs of operating from Rome, which no doubt entered into the investors' calculations.

ART's migration to the Middle East may presage the rise of regional broadcasters that are actually based in the region. The station's decision to relocate to Cairo was made easier by its lack of a strong news operation, giving it less fear of governmental interference in its operations. Whether the relocation will affect ART's tone or broadcasting style is unclear; in any event, the station is perceived as the "most Arab" of the broadcasters that provide a "bouquet" of channels to subscribers. Being close to that subscriber base will presumably help to promote that image.

OTHER CHANNELS

The above profiles do not constitute a comprehensive listing of all of the satellite television channels available in the Arab world, but rather a survey of the most important of them. A number of state-run channels have a following in the region, including the Egyptian Satellite Channel (which now has several channels), Dubai TV, and Future Television (which is private but owned by Prime Minister Rafiq al-Hariri of Lebanon). CNN also has a loyal viewership in the region, as does French broadcaster Canal TV, especially in francophone North Africa. Recently, Libya, Iraq, and even Mauritania have sought to join the ranks of those countries with satellite channels. The impetus for change, however, is coming from the channels profiled above, and far more viewers tune in to their programming.

TECHNOLOGY ISSUES

Communications satellites revolutionized the coverage of world news in the 1960s and 1970s. With satellites, television stations could transmit images filmed the same day to viewers halfway around the world, rather than wait the better part of a week for a film canister to make the trek from the field to a broadcast studio. In the 1980s, home viewers began to tap into the stream of information and images shooting through the sky. The requisite antennas were huge—as much as ten feet across—but the pictures were crystal-clear, and the variety of programming available far exceeded what ordinary, or terrestrial, broadcasters were providing. In isolated areas where few terrestrial broadcasters existed, enormous satellite dishes began to dot the landscape. High-powered satellites in the early 1990s shrunk the size of the requisite dishes to something on the order of a meter across, and advances in technology, lower satellite orbits, and in some cases new broadcast frequencies are driving dish size down to 50 centimeters (20 inches) across or smaller.

A second transition underway in the industry, the use of digital transmission signals, has the advantage of multiplying by seven or more the number of channels that can be broadcast from each satellite transponder. The resulting images and sound are of very high quality, much like a compact disc. Digital broadcasting holds out the promise of multiplying programming choices and improving reception quality from existing satellite slots, although it does little to rein-in the costs of producing programming. In addition, digital broadcasting requires more expensive equipment than analog broadcasts, especially on the receiving end, which may reduce its popularity in some quarters. Orbit has shifted to digital broadcasts for its programming, and several other stations either have done so or plan to.

The third transition is the rapid expansion in the number of satellites that can carry broadcast programming. Communications satellites were a rarity in the early 1970s, but escalating demand, combined with advances in rocket and satellite technology, have led to a rapid multiplication in their numbers. Arab regional broadcasters have a choice of transmitting from one of the Arabsat satellites (owned by an Arab League consortium), an Intelsat satellite (owned by an international consortium), the Egyptian-owned Nilesat (launched in April 1998), or one of several other options. The rapid spread of satellites over the Middle East also holds the promise of facilitating other communications options, including telephone, radio, and the internet.

One change on the horizon that may cut into the market for satellite broadcasts is the rise of so-called "wireless cable"[36] operations in several Arab countries. Such a system operates in Qatar and parts of Egypt and is slated to operate in Saudi Arabia in December 1998. Wireless cable is essentially a rebroadcast of television programming in a small area. It offers the wide variety of choice characteristic of cable and satellite programming (and can be either digital or analog), but it does not require a satellite dish. On the other hand, wireless cable injects an intermediary (generally, the state) between the broadcaster and the viewer, and this intermediary can potentially censor programming thought to be objectionable. Although wireless cable systems may reinject state control into television viewing, such systems have been scarce until now, and they are therefore not a major factor in Middle Eastern broadcasting. When Saudi Arabia's system is up and running—and the launch date has been pushed back for years—the experiment in the Arab world's most valuable advertising market bears close watching.

JON B. ALTERMAN

SUMMARY

Whereas few satellite television stations have found a way to make money in the new medium, the number of Arabs watching satellite programs grows steeply every year. The new viewers are drawn to the attractive programming, the relatively free debate, and the additional viewing choice satellite programming provides. Some states have tried to jump into the satellite television race for viewers, but most of the popular stations are privately owned and independent of state control. Saudi capital plays a preeminent role in financing the private stations, however, and criticism of the Saudi government remains out-of-bounds for broadcasters. With that caveat aside, though, the satellite stations have been breaking down censorship barriers and creating a competition for viewers in what until recently was a staid, state-owned media environment.

NOTES

1   It is not uncommon, for example, for the national evening news broadcast in an Arab country to begin with a silent ten-minute shot of the head of state greeting a large delegation of visiting dignitaries by kissing each one on both cheeks.

2   Estimates of access to satellite broadcasts come from Prof. Hussein Amin, American University in Cairo, and others. "Access" is an estimate based on the number of dishes multiplied by a factor estimating the number of people who watch television on each dish (generally, about six). Khawola Al-Otaiky of the Kuwaiti International Information Center estimates Egyptian viewership at only 2 million, or less than 4 percent of the population. Hala Kaloti, "Arab Satellite TV Channels Prove Ineffective," Inter Press Service, November 10, 1997.

3   Interview with MBC officials in London, March 17, 1998.

4   As is well known, Saudi television waited for several days before reporting that Iraq had invaded Kuwait.

5   Saudi Information Office, Washington, D.C.

6   The founder of MBC, Shaykh Walid al-Ibrahim, told the *Christian Science Monitor* that his inspiration for the station came when he was studying at the University of Oregon at Eugene. He saw a vast difference between Saudi and American programming, and said, "I knew there was definitely a market to be exploited here." Faiza S. Ambah, "Arabs Channel-Surf Past State-Run TV," *Christian Science Monitor,* May 24, 1995, p. 1. Al-Ibrahim told another paper that the idea came to him while at business school at Portland State University. Youssef Ibrahim, "TV Is Beamed at Arabs. The Arabs Beam Back," *New York Times*, March 4, 1992, p. 4.

7   Profile on Orbit's official web page: www.orbit.inet.it/company_profile/

8   The major Arab stations have all invested in state-of-the-art video equipment. Rebecca Hawkes, "Delving into Digital Video," *Middle East Broadcast and Satellites* (March 1998).

9   In 1994, total advertising spending in the Arab world was $900 million, while spending in Israel alone was $800 million. Jihad Khazen in Abdel Bari Atwan and Jihad Khazen, "In the Saudi Pocket," *Index on Censorship 2* (1996), p. 52.

10   Chris Forrester, "Satellite Strength: Middle East Broadcasts from on High," *Middle East Broadcast and Satellites* (March 1998).

11   Ibid.

12   Ibid.

13   "Free-to-air" refers to programs broadcast without encoding, which can therefore be viewed without proprietary equipment, monthly subscription fees, and the like.

14   MBC currently has correspondents in every Arab country except Sudan and Libya, in addition to correspondents in the United States, France, Belgium, Sweden, Denmark, Germany, Italy, Bosnia, Russia, and India.

15   Interview with Pierre Ghanem, London, March 16, 1998.

16   OR Productions, run by Othman al-Omeir and Abdel Rahman al-Rashed, produced the Desert Storm documentary series. Until recently, al-Omeir was editor in chief of *al-Sharq al-Awsat*, and al-Rashed was editor in chief of *al-Majalla*. Al-Rashed now edits both publications.

17   "Six Years Later, Gulf War Is Seen Through Arab Eyes," Associated Press, May 12, 1997.

18   Ibid.

19   The lack of cinemas, theaters, and other forms of public entertainment in Saudi Arabia puts an emphasis on entertainment in the home, and in practice that often involves watching television. According to a survey of 495 Saudi adults conducted in December 1995 and January 1996, 64 percent had access to a satellite dish and spent an average of 21 hours per week watching television, and 72 percent had access to video cassette recorders and spent an additional six hours a week on average watching programs on them. Khalid Marghalani, Philip Palmgreen, and Douglas A. Boyd, "The Utilization of Direct Satellite Broadcasting (DBS) in Saudi Arabia," *Journal of Broadcasting & Electronic Media* 42, no. 3 (Summer 1998), p. 304.

20   Report in *Video Age*, cited in Robert Trevelyan and Diarmid O'Sullivan, "Saudi Investors Extend Their Reach," *Middle East Economic Digest*, August 15, 1997, p. 2.

21   According to one report, al-Jazeera received a $137 million grant from the Qatari government. Despite that, it aired the views of jailed dissidents accusing the Qatari government of torture. Faiza Saleh Ambah, "TV Channel Captivates Arab Viewers," Associated Press, June 22, 1998.

22 "Arabsat and Another Kind of Pornography," *al-Jazira*, March 13, 1998, translated as "Saudi Writer Attacks Qatari Satellite Station Programs," in FBIS-NES-98-078 (Foreign Broadcast Information Service–Near East and South Asia, Daily Report online), March 19, 1998.

23 Interview with Faisal al-Qasim, *al-Sharq al-Awsat TV* magazine (in Arabic), March 16, 1998, p. 7.

24 *CIA World Factbook* 1997, online at www.odci.gov/cia/publications/factbook/qa.html.

25 In the *al-Sharq al-Awsat TV* interview, Faisal al-Qasim, on p. 6, states that accusations of government intervention in editorial policy "have absolutely no basis in fact."

26 LBC program guide, online at www.lbci.com.lb.

27 "Al-Asad's Nephew Reportedly Launching TV Satellite Network," *al-Watan al-Arabi*, June 6, 1997, p. 16, translated in FBIS-NES-97-159, June 8, 1997.

28 Roula Khalaf, "Doctor Who Wants Democratic Arab TV," *Financial Times*, May 1, 1998, p. 4.

29 See "Syria: Dismissal of Rifaat al-Asad the Announcement of an Old Decision," *al-Wasat* (in Arabic), February 16, 1998, p. 22. A Jordanian weekly tabloid made a similar argument: see "Report Probes al-Asad–Brother 'Struggle,'" *Shihan*, February 28, 1998, p. 13, translated in FBIS-NES-98-061, March 2, 1998.

30 "Arab Governments Use the Weapons of Satellite Channels in Their Political and Media Wars," *al-Quds al-Arabi* (in Arabic), March 18, 1998, p. 1.

31 According to a reporter who closely follows the Arab satellite broadcasting industry, independent estimates put Orbit's subscriber base closer to 80,000. Chris Forrester, "Digital Platforms in the Middle East," *Transnational Broadcasting Studies*, online at www.tbsjournal.com/html/digital_platforms.html.

32 John Tagliabue, "Tapping the Power of Satellite TV," *New York Times,* April 15, 1996, p. D1.

33 Presumably, hotels pay a reduced rate for Orbit, and hotels represent a large portion of the "viewer base" of 180,000.

34 "Saudi Businessman Sells 37.5 Pct Stake in MBC," Reuters, June 7, 1994.

35 Faiza S. Ambah, "Arabs Channel-Surf Past State-Run TV," *Christian Science Monitor,* May 24, 1995, p. 1.

36 Wireless cable is, technically, a microwave multidirectional system, or MMDS.

Chapter 4

The Internet

Few stories have gripped the world press as strongly as the spread of the internet in the 1990s. Sensing that the easy, instantaneous, and inexpensive exchange of text and pictures will be a powerful force in remaking the world in the late twentieth century, journalists have rushed to tout the promise of the new medium, at times exaggerating its current importance. The Arab world has joined in the global enthusiasm for the internet. It is available in almost every Arab country, and the number of users grows monthly. Every Thursday *al-Hayat* runs a full page on computer topics. *PC Magazine*'s Middle and Near East Edition sells tens of thousands of copies. Thirty-four daily Arab newspapers maintain pages on the worldwide web, many of them post the complete text of their daily editions, and only one charges for the privilege of reading it. Nongovernmental organizations throughout the Middle East—charities, opposition political movements, and even Hizballah—have a strong internet presence, relying both on electronic mail (e-mail) and web pages to exchange information. An increasing number of Arab governments are also establishing a presence on the worldwide web; among the most active has been Egypt, with several web pages for the State Information Service, the presidency, the Ministry of Foreign Affairs, and a large number of additional government organs. Jordan has also been active establishing a web presence: Its internal security apparatus maintains a web page, as does Queen Noor.

INTERNET ACCESS

The sudden burst of the internet on public consciousness in the Middle East raises a number of interesting questions, among them who is using the internet, how, and to what effect. Numbers of internet users in a given country are notoriously hard to determine. They are even more difficult to divine in environments in which many people's access may be via public computers in internet cafes or semi-public ones at universities and research organizations. Is "internet use" defined by the ownership of an e-mail account? Is it defined by "surfing" the web in a public place without having an individual account? How does one calculate the number of users of shared accounts?

One of the most recent estimates of internet usage in the Middle East, made in the spring of 1998, claims a total of 1.35 million Middle Eastern users. Turkey is estimated to lead the region with some 600,000 users out of a population of 63.5 million; Israel is second, with about 300,000 total users, but with a population of only 5.5 million, slightly more than 5 percent of Israelis are online. The Arab country with the highest total of users is the United Arab Emirates (UAE), with 88,552 estimated users, followed by Egypt with 61,021. Qatar leads the Arab countries in the proportion of its population that uses the internet, with 3.10 percent.[1] If one estimates 129.5 million internet users worldwide in June 1998, the Middle East as a whole contains less than one percent of the world population of internet users, and the Arab world some three-tenths of a percent.[2]

All of these numbers are highly fluid. One leading firm estimates that the internet grew by more than 50 percent worldwide in the first six months of 1998, and by 84 percent through 1997.[3] Arab use in general parallels these gains, although according to survey data, growth in some of the Gulf markets, like Kuwait and Bahrain, seems to lag a bit. The computer market overall in the Arab world is growing at an annual rate of 20 percent, and in some countries, like Lebanon, Egypt, and Saudi Arabia, it is growing at 50 percent to 60 percent per year.[4] Some sort of internet service is available in every Arab country but Iraq.[5] Saudi Arabia will soon offer full internet access to its residents, which will no doubt boost Arab numbers significantly.

OBSTACLES TO ACCEPTANCE

A number of obstacles have hindered widespread acceptance of the internet in the Arab world. The first is language. By far the primary language of the internet is English, accounting for an overwhelming majority of home pages on the worldwide web and by far the bulk of e-mail traffic as well.[6] In a world constructed on a backbone using a Roman alphabet, Arab users who are not familiar with English are disadvantaged. Initially, Arabic texts on the internet were loaded as graphics files—that is, users essentially received a photograph of the text rather than the text itself. Doing so made such pages relatively easy to display but very difficult to search, as the words were not conveyed as searchable text but as an image.[7] More recently, software advances have created widely available browsers that can reproduce Arabic text. Such browsers read normally unused Roman characters—like Å, ÿ, and ø—and display them as Arabic letters. There are still bugs in some of the programs, and some require the use of an Arabic computer operating system,[8] but for the most part this hurdle seems to be cleared. Still, according to a survey of Arab internet users released in March 1998, 40 percent could not read Arabic on their browsers.[9]

Even when the problem of representing text is overcome, however, there remains the problem that the bulk of the information available on the internet is in English. The value of the worldwide web lies in the wealth of its resources, and there are few in Arabic. Internet search engines are generally optimized to run in English, and being nearly invisible to most search engines is a major liability. In the last two years, a number of Arabic search engines have begun to emerge, making it easier for Arabic-speakers to find Arabic information on the worldwide web. Yet, these Arabic search engines cannot *create* Arabic material, and that remains scarce, both in absolute terms and especially when compared to English-language material. The dilemma, then, is that the presence of Arabic material will depend on how much the Arab world embraces the web, and yet that will depend at least in part on how much Arabic material is there. At the present time, a large number of governmental and nongovernmental organizations in the Arab world have web sites, and a preponderance of those sites are in English, even when their intended audience is an Arab one.

With the general integration of e-mail functions and web browsers in the last several years, Arabic-enabled browsers now allow the exchange of Arabic-text messages without transliteration into the Roman alphabet. Like Arabic web pages, however, acceptance of Arabic for messaging depends on the widespread use of Arabic for messaging. For the time being, Roman alphabets are the standard, although the explosive growth of the internet worldwide and in Arab countries could turn that around in a matter of months.

By most standards, internet connectivity is expensive in the Middle East. Egypt has more than thirty internet service providers (ISPs), and a single account with full internet access runs between $30 and $35 per month for about thirty hours of time, plus an initial start-up fee and a government tax of 10 percent. In Bahrain, where the government phone company is the sole internet provider, fees run about $40 per month plus $0.25 per minute.[10] In the UAE, the country with the largest number of residents with internet access, the price is closest to American levels: $23 for fourteen hours of use, and $1.60 for each additional hour.[11] Added to this are the costs of equipment and software. The former must be imported and is taxed as a luxury item in most countries; the latter is expensive but often pirated (and thus low-cost or cost-free, albeit illegal). Combining all these costs, a potential user in the region must have access to $3,000 or more, a sum that keeps the internet out of the hands of the vast bulk of the population in most Arab countries. Even where internet cafes exist (Jordan, Egypt, and many of the Gulf states), they are relatively expensive: about $6.50 per hour in Kuwait, about $7 per hour in Ramallah, and $4 per hour in Cairo. Whereas such a price may appeal to highly Westernized elites, it is beyond the resources of most residents, especially considering the steep learning curve that non-computer literate users must confront.

Students and some businesspeople can escape the high cost structure that typifies internet use. Like their American counterparts, Arab universities have been among the first institutions in most countries to connect to the internet. Yet, access in universities can be restricted. Public terminals may be severely overused, modem connections may be nonexistent, and service may be unreliable. As the internet is still thought of in many places as a benefit for faculty rather than as a resource for students, many Arab students become aware of the internet while studying at a university but lack the opportunities to learn anything more than the most rudimentary skills. Businesspeople may also enjoy internet access at work, and an increasing number of Arab businesses are finding the internet is a cost-effective alternative to phone, fax, and printing. Still, narrowly restricted business use of the internet is unlikely to have the broadly transformative effects that internet enthusiasts foresee, unless those who are exposed to the internet at work feel moved to get personal accounts.

The people in the Arab world who do use the internet generally fit a rather narrow profile. According to a survey by *Arab Internet World* magazine that appeared in March 1998, the average internet user in the Arab world is a 29-year-old male with a university education. Arab users are significantly younger than their American counterparts, whose average age is 36. Another difference is the minuscule number of female internet users in the Arab world: a mere 4 percent of surveyed users. About half of Arab users reported using the internet at work, and most of them worked for large organizations (generally universities or governments). In private-sector organizations, access rates were low, ranging from 17 percent in computer- and internet-related companies, to a mere 2 percent in banking and insurance.[12]

Obstacles to widespread access to the internet are not all on the consumer side. Many countries lack the infrastructure to allow widescale data transmission over their phone lines. In some cases, the local phone lines and phone switching networks are insufficient to permit a high level of traffic. In many others, there is not enough space on the lines connecting to the internet and the rest of the world.[13] Merely getting a phone line can take years in many countries, although in recent years wait times have dropped substantially. A possible work-around to the shortage of bandwidth—the electronic "space" required to pass data back and forth—is the use of communications satellites for the purpose. Such satellites use regular phone lines to send outgoing commands, but send the resultant data back via satellite. ZakSat is the first company in the Arab world to offer such a service; it uses the AsiaSat II satellite to provide service in Egypt, Jordan, Lebanon, and Kuwait. In April 1998, Prince al-Walid bin Talal of Saudi Arabia invested $200 million in Teledesic, a company that aims to do much the same worldwide.

Many countries—Bahrain, the UAE, and soon Saudi Arabia—pass all internet traffic through a single government-controlled gateway before it leaves the country. Governments can use the gateway to ban access to certain sites, and also to monitor e-mail communication. Although there is anecdotal evidence suggesting that some governments have, on occasion, resorted to the former, human rights activists in the Arab world and in the United States are unaware of any punitive government actions taken on account of intercepted e-mail messages. It is unclear whether this will change as e-mail becomes more prevalent and government intelligence services become more comfortable with the technology.[14]

PROMISE AND THREAT

The internet certainly has seized the interest of governments throughout the region—interest rather than enthusiasm, because they regard the internet as both promising and threatening for the region. The ambivalence was nicely captured in an address delivered by Ibrahim Nafie, the editor in chief of Cairo's semi-official daily newspaper, *al-Ahram*. In his opening speech to a marketing conference in May 1998, Nafie told the audience:

> As we speak, the internet is creating a new form of collective thinking that opens new horizons for the imagination and new potentials for adventure and work. For the first time it is in our power to imagine a universal civilization. It is capable not only of reforming the national economies, but also reforming identities and changing sentiments on the local and regional levels. The internet is not merely a door-knocker for the advertising industry. It is part of the technological innovation originated in the North and which has engrossed the South, overwhelming its mind and integrating it into its cultural and values system.[15]

Nowhere has ambivalence over the internet been more public than in Syria, where Bashar al-Asad, the president's son and heir apparent, has been calling for increased access to computers and the internet. The younger Asad was studying to be an ophthalmologist in Britain before the death of his older brother in a 1994 car accident that caused him to return home and prepare himself someday to rule Syria. Many observers believe that he brings to Syria a new outlook borne of his experience in the West—less xenophobic and less mistrustful of change. Bashar al-Asad tries to push forward a more technology-friendly agenda through his position as the president of the Syrian Computer Society, an organization started by his late brother Basil in 1989. Pushing a pro-computer agenda is difficult in Syria, though, because the constituency is so small and the security forces so powerful. In October 1997, there were estimated to be 35,000 personal computers in all of Syria[16]—two for every 1,000 people—and many of them are presumably older machines that are useless for running modern applications.

Bashar al-Asad seems to be pursuing a two-pronged strategy in his effort to introduce the internet and computers more generally into Syrian life. On the one hand, he states openly and often that any such introduction will be carefully controlled and gradual.[17] In November 1997 a small pilot project began to allow some Syrians internet access—the numbers were kept down to about 400 participants, and the project slated to run only six months.[18]

The other component is to develop Arab resources on the internet. Syrian programmers and technicians have been developing Arabic search engines, databases, and data to provide a counterweight to "propaganda opposed to the cause of Arab nationalism" for Arab net surfers.[19] The idea here is that the internet is full of anti-Syrian propaganda that is growing exponentially, and Syrians had better establish a presence to counteract it. This attitude was made clear in the press coverage of a speech that appeared in February 1998 in the regime mouthpiece *Tishrin*. The presenter, Dr. Imad Mustafa, began by stating that 92 percent of the countries of the world offer internet service to their citizens, and then discussed the importance of the medium as a means of communication. The bulk of the lecture, however, presented the results of an internet survey performed earlier in the month. Mustafa stated that 128,000 Israeli organizations and individuals have sites on the internet. Perhaps more disturbing to him, Mustafa said his researchers located 1,439,664 documents "which deal with the Syrian aspect of the Arab–Israeli conflict." Among the first 200, "56 percent were written by Israeli groups and individuals, 18 percent by Zionist organizations outside of Israel, 17 percent by mostly U.S. government organizations, 6 percent by tourism companies and organizations, and 3 percent by individuals." Regarding the Golan, 71 percent of the files found "are very hostile to Syria, 12 percent are typical informative ones that appear to be innocent but conceal malicious points of view, [and] 17 percent were put on the network by Israeli organizations which outwardly call for peace with Syria and the rest of the Arabs, but in reality seek something else."[20] In each case, the totals given equal 100 percent—that is, the internet currently contains no material that is benign to Syrian interests.

Among Mustafa's suggested responses to the prevailing situation were, on the one hand, to provide widespread internet access for Syrians, and on the other, to "assign certain groups to check all that is placed on the internet on Syria and confront it by giving explanations or correcting distorted information."[21]

Continued sparring over internet access in Syria surfaced again in May 1998, during a national festival sponsored by the Syrian Computer Society. At that forum, division between two ranks was clear. According to the pan-Arab daily *al-Hayat,* those ranks consisted of those "afraid of information sciences [*al-ma'alumatiya*] and opening the country to the world of the internet because it will lead to cultural penetration," and "those calling strongly for the entry of the world of information sciences and dissemination of the internet to citizens, arguing that 'Arab culture is strong and will not tremble and will not risk cultural domination.'"[22] Despite the enthusiastic support of the president's son, cautious bureaucrats appear to be triumphing over computer enthusiasts, arousing frustration among the latter. In a stark criticism of the Syrian government, the paper quoted Imad Mustafa as saying in one discussion group, "Syria sends experts abroad to learn about information sciences, but the problem is that administrative decision makers are blind to information sciences and cannot make appropriate decisions."[23]

Debate in Saudi Arabia has been somewhat less public. According to individuals familiar with the preparations for introducing the internet, the Saudis have concentrated in part on establishing the requisite telecommunications infrastructure for widespread internet access,[24] but even more so on establishing a method of controlling access to objectionable websites. When the network is opened, all domestic service will connect to the outside world via a "supernode" that is government-controlled and designed to "prevent access to sites containing politically, socially, or culturally sensitive material.[25] A further concern is how the financial rewards of providing internet service will be divided. According to the most comprehensive technical study available of internet use in the Persian Gulf, the desire of several parties to maintain a monopoly over the new services has been an additional brake on rapid development.[26]

Currently, direct internet access is available to about one in one thousand Saudis, and only for official business.[27] A large number of Saudis—as many as 30,000—maintain accounts overseas and dial internationally to access them.[28] One estimate is that half of the Saudi accounts overseas are in Bahrain. The magnitude of the phenomenon is demonstrated by the fact that in its survey of internet usage, the UAE-based DIT Group lumps Saudi Arabia and Bahrain together in the same market.[29] With about 500,000 computers already in the kingdom, the Saudi organization responsible for planning and implementing internet connectivity predicts an immediate demand for 30,000 accounts, and a subsequent demand for as many as 90,000 more within the first year.[30] Such growth would catapult Saudi Arabia into the position of the Arab world's leader in providing internet access, from its current position trailing the pack.

One of the interesting developments arising from the internet in the Arab world is its growing role in promoting intra-Arab trade. On the one hand, the internet facilitates communication between businesses in different countries. More important in the short term, however, is the extent to which the disparities between countries in their populations' familiarity with the internet has led to a lively intra-Arab trade in internet expertise and services. One of the larger companies that designs web pages commercially and also maintains several sites of its own is Arabia Online, a Jordanian-based company in which Prince al-Walid bin Talal bought a 50 percent share in the spring of 1998. On the design side, the company has a large list of clients in Jordan and throughout the Persian Gulf. Because of the nature of the medium, design products can be shipped instantaneously over the internet, so the physical location where the design is done is irrelevant. The company charges several thousand dollars for a few days' work. Designers are well-paid by Jordanian standards—about $700 per month—but earn far less than what comparable workers would earn in the wealthier and more expensive Gulf.

On the site maintenance side, Arabia Online runs a number of "gateway" sites that contain their own content as well as links to other sites. Like gateway sites in the United States (Yahoo.com and Netscape.com are two of the better known ones), the company makes money by selling advertising and running promotions on its pages. Arabia Online runs not only a flagship site by the same name, but also a dedicated news site, Akhbar.com (*akhbar* means "news" in Arabic), and sites for the UAE, Jordan, Qatar, Oman, Lebanon, Saudi Arabia, and the Palestinians. Sites for other countries are in the works, although it seems unlikely that projected efforts in Libya, Sudan, and Iraq will come online soon.

Summary

A number of obstacles exist to the widespread acceptance of the internet in the Arab world, among them language, cost, and computer illiteracy. Governments also remain concerned at opening up an unregulated world of information to their populations. This ambivalence is most visible in Syria, where the president's son is waging an often losing battle to increase internet access. The introduction of widespread internet access in the region's most important market, Saudi Arabia—planned for December 1998—will be an important test of the demand for internet services and the efficacy of government control over access to information.

Notes

1   See www.nua.ie/surveys/how_many_online/index.html, and underlying pages; for population, see www.odci.gov/cia/publications/factbook/country-frame.html.

2   See www.nua.ie/surveys/how_many_online/index.html, and underlying pages.

3   See www.nua.ie/surveys/analysis/domain_survey_analysis.html. Although the Nua study is not explicit, presumably Palestinian internet users are counted as part of the Israeli total. The major Palestinian internet service providers hook up to Israeli ISPs before going abroad.

4   "Technology and Information: The Arab Spends Twenty Dollars and the American Three Hundred Dollars," *al-Wasat* (in Arabic), April 20, 1998, p. 38.

5   The standard survey of internet domain names is done by a firm called Net Wizards. The results of the company's surveys can be found at www.nw.com/zone/WWW/top.html.

6   According to a survey of home pages published in June 1997 by the Internet Society, 82.3 percent of home pages are in English. The next-most-common language was German, with 4.0 percent. See www.isoc.org:8080/palmares.html.

7   The primary examples of web pages that place Arabic text online as images are those of the Arabic newspapers. Some use simple graphics to transmit individual articles; others use Adobe Acrobat, which transmits a high-resolution image of a complete page of the paper, but one that is somewhat difficult to print or manipulate.

8   Windows 95 has a special Arabic version.

9   Yasser I. Elguindy, "IAW Profiles Arab Internet Market," *Tradeline*, March 6, 1998.

10   See www.batelco.com.bh/internet/general.htm.

11   See www.emirates.net.ae/rates.html. The start-up fee in the UAE is about $55.

12   Elguindy, "IAW Profiles Arab Internet Market."

13   The problem most Arabs have in accessing the internet occurs because there is

not enough bandwidth for them to download web pages based outside the region. The bandwidth required to send commands and transfer intra-regional information is relatively small.

14 Issues of monitoring and censorship are discussed more completely in chapter 5, below.

15 Hassan 'Amir, "Conference in Cairo Explores the Art of Selling," *al-Wasat* (in Arabic), May 25, 1998, p. 35.

16 Ibrahim Hamidi and Rania Ismail, "Bashar al-Asad: We Are Working toward Increasing Arab Information in the Electronic Marketplace," *al-Hayat* (in Arabic), October 12, 1997, p. 10.

17 See, for example, Ibrahim Hamidi and Rania Ismail, "Asad's Son to *al-Hayat*: The Internet Is a Double-Edged Sword," *al-Hayat* (in Arabic), October 12, 1997, p. 1.

18 Unclassified cable #007391, U.S. Embassy in Damascus to the U.S. Information Agency, December 11, 1997.

19 Hamidi and Ismail, "Asad's Son."

20 Husayn al-Ibrahim, "The Internet and Informatics in the Arab–Israeli Conflict," *Tishrin,* February 23, 1998, p. 7, translated as "Syrian Lecture on Import of Internet in Peace," in FBIS-NES-98-060 (Foreign Broadcast Information Service–Near East and South Asia, Daily Report online), March 1, 1998.

21 Ibid.

22 Ibrahim Hamidi, "Confrontation in Syria between Two Generations, One of Them Arguing that the Internet 'Harms the Complexion,'" *al-Hayat* (in Arabic), May 4, 1998, p. 1.

23 Ibid.

24 A $4 billion upgrade of the Saudi telephone system is scheduled to be completed in 2001. Grey Burkhart et al., *The Global Diffusion of the Internet Project: An Initial Inductive Study*, (MOSAIC Group, 1998), pp. 209–210. Available online at www.agsd.com/gdi97/gdi97.html.

25 Robert Trevelyan, "Saudi Arabia's Reluctant Passage," *Middle East Economic Digest*, June 26, 1998, p. 3.

26 Burkhart et al., *The Global Diffusion of the Internet Project*, pp. 211, 216.

27 Ibid., p. 212.

28 "Connecting with the Saudis," *Arabia Online*, July 2, 1998, www.arabiaonline.com/content/tech/7_98/saudi_2.7.98.

29 See, for example, www.nua.ie/surveys/how_many_online/m_east.html.

30 Trevelyan, "Saudi Arabia's Reluctant Passage," p. 3.

Chapter 5

Analysis and Prospects

I t is difficult to enumerate the consequences of the information revolution described in the preceding chapters, both in terms of present-day conditions and prospects for future change. The rather sudden increase in ease of transferring data across and within national borders is at the center of global changes; this change is much more marked in the Arab world because so many barriers to information exchange previously existed.

CONTROL OF INFORMATION

Censorship

Nineteenth-century Arab governments established censorship laws to exist alongside their new presses, and government restrictions on speech continued throughout the colonial era and into the independence period. Present-day print media censorship exists in many forms, from excising offensive articles from newspapers and magazines to banning printed materials. Governments can censor the broadcast media by jamming standard radio and television transmissions. Perhaps the most strenuous censorship in many countries occurs with audio cassettes and videotapes sent through the mail. Mindful that the Iranian revolution was aided by smuggled-in cassettes of Ayatollah Ruhollah Khomeini's sermons, many Arab governments review recorded materials in their entirety before forwarding them to the addressee months later.

There are generally four grounds for censorship in the Arab world today. The first has to do with the bounds of political debate. Whereas every

Arab country has some degree of free debate, in each there are "red lines" that cannot be crossed. These red lines often have to do with Islamist opposition forces. Saudi Arabia is particularly sensitive to anything that might promote the views of any political opposition, and Egypt vigorously guards against allowing the views of convicted terrorist and cleric Omar Abdel Rahman (currently in detention in the United States) from circulating in that country. In other countries, like Bahrain, the red lines generally involve support for the country's internal Shi'a opposition movements.[1] A red line in many countries involves criticism of other Arab countries that might adversely affect relations between the criticized state and the host state.

A second and related taboo is criticism of a country's rulers or their families. From Morocco to Iraq, rulers may not be criticized by name in the domestic media. In Morocco, the king is colloquially referred to as *huwwa* ("he") so as to provide plausible deniability for any possible slight. In an incident that raised eyebrows in the Arab world, Hosni Mubarak's sons successfully sued the regional newspaper *al-Sharq al-Awsat* in connection with a story purporting to reveal details of their personal corruption. In what many regional press observers saw as a one-two punch, the brothers succeeded in getting the story killed, and then sued for damages on the grounds that, because the story never came out, allegations made in promotions for the story were unsubstantiated. Bahraini law prohibits "making any criticism of or blaming the Amir for any act of government or holding him responsible for any act."[2] In most countries, political cartoons depict only secondary political figures—prime ministers or allegorical governmental bureaucrats—because depicting the actual leader in a critical light is so clearly out of bounds.

A third taboo has to do with writing of a religious nature that might cause undue dissension in a country. Islam is the majority religion in every country in the Arab world, but there remains disagreement within and between countries regarding what the proper practice of Islam requires. Within the generally acceptable bounds of discussion are debates over the nature of Islamic finance, cultural conflict with Western secularism, and the role of women in the family and in the workplace.[3] What are generally barred are discussions that seek to delegitimize Muslim groups or that incite violence against religious minorities. This is often a floating line, and it is most clearly crossed when Islamist partisans start tossing around the concepts of apostasy (*ridda*) or disbelief (*kufr*) to describe groups or individuals whose views they oppose.[4] Whereas governments in the region often try to appropriate Islam to legitimize their own rule, they are vigilant in guarding against the possibility that some would use Islam to delegitimize either the government itself or groups in the general population.

The fourth taboo has to do with social and sexual mores. As with religious debates, the boundaries of discussion and depiction vary from country to country. The most common denominator is a regional ban on pornography, but to varying degrees other aspects of sexual relations (heterosexual and homosexual) are also proscribed. Social mores drawn more broadly—such as intrafamily relations—are of varying sensitivity depending on the country and the issue, but they are certainly of interest to government censors. The guiding principle seems in many ways not so much to ban because of the nature of the materials themselves, but rather to ban those materials that are likely to cause (or have caused) offense among the domestic clergy or political opposition figures.

Challenges to Censorship

The transnational media tend to undermine the censorship described above. Print publications are still relatively easy to censor using established procedures and institutions, but exerting control over satellite broadcasts is considerably less direct and less effective. Censorship over the internet is more difficult still, and perhaps the easiest to circumvent, because many of those who want to circumvent the restrictions are more technically savvy than those who want to keep the restrictions in place. Each will be discussed in turn below.

Print censorship has by far the longest history in the region, and procedures and institutions exist for its execution. Domestic papers can be closed by government decree for printing information deemed inappropriate or harmful. In September 1998, a new press and publications law took effect in Jordan that contains broad restrictions on press freedom in the kingdom. Attacked by members of the Jordanian press and international human rights groups for the vagueness of the law's proscriptions and the harshness of its penalties, Information Minister Nasser Judeh defended the move by stating that the government favored a "soft implementation" of the law.[5] Such a soft implementation could swiftly turn draconian, however, at the government's whim.

Censorship can also be imposed on foreign publications. Governments can impound or ban single issues of international newspapers and magazines to keep the report of an event out of the local market, or they may ban them for a period of days or weeks to punish a publisher. When this

author lived in Egypt, from 1992 to 1995, publications including interviews with Shaykh Omar Abdel Rahman were systematically banned, but
there did not appear to be a long-term policy of punishing publications
that ran such materials. In Jordan, copies of London-based *al-Quds al-
Arabi* were confiscated thirty-seven times in the first four months of 1998,
leading to an indefinite (but short-lived) complete ban on the paper in May.[6]
The *Jordan Times* quoted the *al-Quds al-Arabi* correspondent in Amman
as saying that the proximate cause was articles concerning the government's
relationship with Islamist parties in the run-up to the November 1997 elections.[7] The government complained that the paper was "distorting the image of Jordan abroad and harming ties between Jordan and friendly countries
and insulting the country's dignity,"[8] and that it persisted "in publishing
reports and analyses that went against the simplest rules of professional
conduct and objectivity."[9]

Nontraditional methods of information transfer are posing new challenges to government censors. Viewers with satellite dishes can watch international television broadcasts independent of an individual government's
wishes to censor or control viewing habits.[10] The internet has also under-
mined print censorship in many ways. When *al-Quds al-Arabi* was banned
in Jordan, the newspaper took out advertisements in several Jordanian papers inviting readers to read the banned issues over the internet, where
they available for free.

Although governments can and do use available technology to block
access to certain internet sites, in doing so they are playing a game of catch-
up. The contents of web pages can be faxed or electronically mailed (e-
mailed) to a censoring country from accounts outside its borders. Those pages
can be sent anonymously, encrypted, or both, thus obscuring both the web
pages' origin and content (for more on both, see below). Web pages themselves can be located at a swiftly changing series of locations, requiring
studious effort for governments to stay one step ahead of their publics. Rapid
advances in the ability to convey pictures and audio over the worldwide web
mean that not merely text but live, narrated video can be transferred. Video
and cassette tapes, as well as diskettes, all of which can convey a wealth of
information, can be smuggled in easily. One Arab editor said privately in the
spring of 1998, "The censors are losing heart," and that is surely the case.

According to Arab analysts, it is this fear of losing control over what
the public knows that is slowing the development of the internet in the
Arab world. A cover story in the weekly magazine *al-Wasat* concluded:

> The true problem of the internet for the Arabs is primarily the political problem. There is a fear of completely opening the door to the entrance of unsuitable ideas and premises. Given all the "problems" caused by satellite dishes, there is no need to increase them. There is no doubt that behind the official cautionary Arab lines is a fear of what we can call the "Indonesian phenomenon."[11]

In this context, the recent upsurge in censorship of domestic news in the Arab world—including but not limited to Egypt's banning of several publications incorporated overseas, the dismissal of Adel Hamouda from the editorship of the magazine *Ruz al-Yusef*, and continued censorship of the *Middle East Times*; Jordan's intermittent efforts to raise barriers to publishing periodicals in that country; and Lebanese sensitivity to the political content of television news—appears not to indicate the return of the past so much as it hints at how vastly different the future may be. The great degree of room that the transnational media provide for freedom of expression makes central government policymakers uncomfortable and causes them to censor that which they can. But as the transnational media become more pervasive (a trend that seems irreversible), censorship will become at the same time more costly and less effective. Acting against newspapers and magazines—especially domestically produced ones—is both relatively easy and something that the region's central governments do relatively well. Effectively censoring the flood of information coming in from outside their borders requires a new set of tools that they do not yet have, and that are likely to prove far less effective.

Concomitant with their declining ability to censor news coming into their countries, Arab governments have a decreasing ability to shape that news. Every government but Qatar has an information ministry whose essential task is to mobilize the media—and, through them, the public at large—in support of governmental policies. Information ministries monitor reporters' activities and whereabouts and help to shape (and sometimes wholly shape) the news agenda—both that which they produce for domestic consumption, and that which they allow to be broadcast overseas. The proliferation of news outlets—traditional news outlets as well as e-mail newsgroups, web pages, and a host of other information "products"—makes that job much more difficult. News can leak out of individual countries from a vast number of sources, and it can then leak back into the countries through any number of outlets. The situation increasingly resembles that in the West, where governments have a "voice but not a veto" concerning what is known about their domestic and external affairs.

Efforts at control extend to the international arena. For example, the Jordanian weekly *al-Sabil* reported in May 1998 that Jordan Television had recently barred news agencies from transmitting via the state-controlled satellite uplink facility any video images of crowds burning Israeli and American flags. The report added that Jordan Television also barred transmission of reports on Hamas and the Islamist dissident Layth Shbaylat.[12] Anecdotal reports from television journalists working in the region suggest that such action is in no way unique to Jordan, and that many governments attempt to exercise similar control. Such constraints can be relatively easily overcome by flying the videotape to another country and broadcasting from there; advances in satellite uplink technology may make central facilities themselves unnecessary in the future.

A third constraint on news coverage is the harassment or imprisonment of journalists. Such measures are generally applied to the domestic press, and they remain a source for concern in the journalistic and human rights communities. On a less physically threatening level, government ministries can cut journalists off from contact with government officials and thus make it very difficult for them to do their jobs. In that way, the process is little different from that practiced in Western democracies. A recent book on White House media operations during Bill Clinton's presidency is full of anecdotes about journalists who were either rewarded or punished professionally as a consequence of the stories they reported.[13]

The three strategies described above—controlling news, shaping news, and harassing journalists—are ones governments are most able to follow domestically. Agreements between governments, however, can extend the reach of an individual government's efforts beyond its borders. Were the Arab governments to agree, they could in effect establish an "information cartel" and punish individuals in any Arab country that violate the interests of any other Arab country. Although such a cartel is theoretically possible, the practical difficulties in winning complete agreement among all of the involved countries, in particular because of their incompatible or competing foreign policy agendas, make such an arrangement unlikely. Regardless, some dominant regional states will find themselves relatively immune from harsh criticism in the regional media even without a cartel.

Indirect Censorship

An oft-repeated theme among many working in the Arabic news media is the influence of Saudi capital in so many of those news outlets. Saudis own a major chunk of all of the privately financed satellite television stations, and they own the major pan-Arab newspapers and magazines. As noted above, Prince al-Walid bin Talal bought a 50 percent share of Arabia Online and made a $200 million investment in the satellite telecommunications firm Teledesic, and presumably other Saudis will make capital investments in future ventures (in addition to the huge venture of wiring Saudi Arabia itself to the internet). Observers find the pervasiveness of Saudi investments troubling, because they believe that the outlets often reflect Saudi interests, to the detriment of others in the region.

On the one hand, these observers point to the fact that the regional news media cater to Saudi concerns. Saudi domestic policy is virtually above any kind of discussion in print or electronic news outlets, and both it and the country's foreign policy are beyond criticism. The most vocal critic of Saudi influence has been Abdel Bari Atwan, the publisher of *al-Quds al-Arabi* and a former editor of *al-Sharq al-Awsat*. Atwan charges:

> Chief among the political taboos is criticizing the ruling family, made up of more than twenty-thousand princes and princesses. Also, criticizing corruption, commission-taking and arms deals. All mention of the state's financial difficulties, or the vast fortunes amassed by some of the princes (reaching into billions of dollars in some cases) brings instant retribution, as well as any criticism of the country's foreign policy or mention of the presence of American forces and bases in Saudi Arabia.[14]

Atwan asserts that the Saudi government has also signed "media protocols" with several Arab ministries of information that essentially amount to nonaggression pacts.[15] As a consequence, it is difficult to find any criticism of the Saudi regime in any of the printed publications of the region.[16]

Among those reconciled to the effects of Saudi censorship on news coverage, former *al-Hayat* editor Jihad al-Khazen admits frankly that his paper overlooks otherwise worthy stories because of the sensibilities of the Saudi government. For example, in 1994 an Egyptian physician working in Saudi Arabia, Dr. Muhammad Kamel Muhammad Khalifa, complained that the Saudi principal of his son's school was sexually abusing Khalifa's son. The doctor was compelled to recant his story and then flogged for having purportedly "lied" to Saudi authorities in the first place.[17] The story became a *cause célèbre* in the Egyptian press, which used the incident as a metaphor for the poor treatment Egyptians believed they received as workers in the kingdom, and became a source of significant tension between the two countries. Khazen explained, "I refused to take the line of the Egyptians or the Saudis. Rather than risk alienating two of the most important countries for the paper, I ignored the whole story . . . I couldn't put what I wanted to in the paper."[18]

Khazen is frank, as well, in admitting that his paper is dependent on access to the Saudi market. A ban in Saudi Arabia costs the paper some $40,000 to $50,000 per day, in part from lost sales but even more so because so much of the paper's advertising is directed at Saudi consumers. Of $13 million in advertising revenues in 1994, $12.5 came from Saudi Arabia, and "without the Saudi market, *al-Hayat* could not survive."[19] *Al-Hayat*'s need to self-censor because of Saudi sensitivities is mirrored in pressrooms throughout the region.

Saudi sensitivities extend to social and religious issues as well, and this is especially evident when it comes to television programming. Egyptians, who for years have produced the bulk of Arabic television and films, have begun to complain about the influence of Saudi mores on their programs. Because the ability to sell programs to Saudi outlets is so important for the financial viability of Egyptian television production companies, new productions tend to meet Saudi demands for modesty and religious propriety. Egyptians complain, however, that Saudi standards are far narrower than Egyptian ones, and that the Saudi influence on Egypt's artistic output is stultifying.[20]

In the realm of indirect censorship, the rich states have far more advantages than the poorer ones. Under the threat of banning or boycott, the generally Levantine and Egyptian producers of news and entertainment are far more accommodating to Gulf Arab opinions than to those of their own homelands. Indeed, taking risks with news coverage of poorer states helps the news outlets, because it gives the impression of rigorous coverage and helps to obscure the fact that some countries and governments are given a "free ride."[21] In this regard, no group has a harder time than the Palestinian Authority (PA), which on the one hand is of interest to a broad spectrum of Arab opinion and on the other has few effective methods to control reporting. The porosity of its border with Israel and aggressive reporting in the Israeli press gives the PA even less freedom of action in restraining press coverage than exists in other governments in the region. The governments of Egypt and Jordan probably rank next on the list of countries with a low level of control over their press coverage. Some countries, like Sudan, are given a bye because they generate little interest; others, like Libya, Syria, and Iraq, rely on extraordinarily strong internal intelligence apparatuses to keep journalists at bay.

The decline in censorship, then, is uneven. Wealthier states are better able to control what crosses into the country from the outside, whereas poorer states must confront the shifts that an inquisitive press and wider freedoms have wrought in national politics.[22] In a way, the poorer states are serving as a sort of laboratory for the effects of press freedom on politics. The international Arab media will be far more aggressive in their coverage of news in the poorer states, and the effects of that aggressive coverage will be felt far more strongly there than in the Gulf. If the experiment goes well (by Gulf standards)—if it does not result in changes in government, an upheaval in societal relationships, or civil or international war—the Gulf States may decrease their current level of censorship. If the experiment goes poorly, then the Gulf states are likely to maintain if not raise the bars to free expression that already exist.

FREEDOM OF COMMUNICATION

Technology has made great strides in enabling freedom of expression, and those strides will only increase. The first step was the telephone, which enabled real-time transmission of information (albeit over lines that could relatively easily be tapped). The advent of the fax machine in the 1980s further increased people's ability to communicate. The internet, web-based telephonics, and the impending arrival of satellite-based mobile telephone systems hold the prospect of making private communication even more widely available.

At this point, all communications can be monitored in some way by governmental organizations. Unencrypted e-mail messages can be read with ease by government officials; all that is required is relatively inexpensive system administration software.[23] Governments can sift through massive amounts of received messages for keywords—in many ways, the computerization of the messages makes them even easier to search. Perhaps to enable this kind of scanning operation, the government of Tunisia has banned the transmission of encrypted messages without official government sanction.[24] Even when messages are encrypted (which has become increasingly easy to do over the internet), an inquisitive observer can note that an encrypted message has been sent, even if the contents of the message are unknown.[25]

Technological innovations have made it much easier to send messages out of a country with anonymity (which some human rights groups and political opposition forces believe they need). Web-based "remailers" strip away the identity of the sender of a message from prying eyes and anonymously e-mail them to the addressee. Security for the sender is enhanced even more if the message is sent from a public or semipublic computer terminal. Although all such activity can be monitored in some way, technological advances give new advantages to individuals seeking privacy.

Telecommunications advances in the next decade will make privacy even easier to maintain under many conditions. The digitization of telephony and data transfer, and the increasing use of international infrastructures to transfer that information, mean that more and more information can be encrypted or transmitted via circuitous routes. It is also part of a pattern in which the amount of information circulating will rise exponentially. The sheer volume of data flowing back and forth will make it more difficult for government agencies to monitor and censor on a global basis (although individuals or groups will still be able to be watched carefully).[26]

RISE OF REGIONAL DEBATE AND REGIONAL IDENTITY

The rise of regional information organs has reinvigorated a sense of common destiny among many in the Arab world. To a great extent, regional print media and television broadcasts have combined to create a regional media market—known to marketers as the "pan-Arab market"—which is becoming increasingly influential.

The regional media market is notable for several reasons. First, it is, in fact, a market. Relying on supply and demand, programming does not simply meet the needs of government broadcasters, but rather actively seeks viewers who enjoy a variety of news and entertainment options. The consequence is an enormous empowerment of the viewership and a dramatic improvement in viewer satisfaction with programming.

Second, regional markets are, indeed, regional. To a great degree, identical programming can be seen throughout the Arab Middle East. Although market-driven programmers direct their broadcasts primarily to groups with high value to advertisers—in the Arab world, generally wealthy Gulf Arabs—the programming itself reaches and influences many throughout the region who may not fit the targeted socioeconomic profile of each station.

Finally, regional broadcasting has created regional news organizations—both in terms of news coverage and delivery—that far surpass what had previously existed. Many of these news organizations are headquartered outside the region, giving them a degree of independence unprecedented in many countries. The consequence is the emergence of a press corps that both remains independent of the agendas of an individual country and seeks an audience that transcends national borders.

The potential results of the regional media market described above are not hard to imagine. In his insightful book *Imagined Communities*, Benedict Anderson makes a persuasive case that two factors controlled the development of national consciousness in state after state in Reformation Europe: commerce and linguistic unity. As printers sought to expand their markets beyond small numbers of Latin-literate elites, they increased their printing in vernacular languages (Luther's *Theses* drove much of the vernacular printing in Germany for decades). In so doing, they created communities of essentially monolingual people who spoke and wrote in similar languages, but whose communications were largely unintelligible to those from outside the region.[27] These communities drew together to form modern nation-states like France, Germany, and Italy.

As suggested in previous chapters, the advent of print in the Middle East occurred after colonial powers had begun to lay down borders. Napoleon brought movable Arabic type to the region as part of his colonial project in Egypt at the dawn of the nineteenth century, and mass printing remained mainly the province of central governments—ones constructed along the lines of Western states—for most of the next hundred years. As a consequence, Arabic printing tended to reinforce barriers between Arabic speakers rather than to suppress them. Over the years, strong state institutions arose that tended to reinforce the separation between the nascent states of the region. One of those institutions was the state censor, which helped to promote the development of a national identity in much the same way that linguistic unity in Europe led to the perception of national identity.

Transnational media, however, alter this equation fundamentally. What is most apparent about the new technologies is that they facilitate the transmission of information independent of distance. Whereas national differences could be maintained in the twentieth century because geography and governmental efforts combined to create distinct markets for information, new technologies make it cheaper, faster, and easier for information to transcend those obstacles to create something much more closely resembling a single market. In that market, the imperative is to create products that enlarge and unite the market rather than those that fracture it. The consequence has been a generally heightened interest in international affairs, which often takes the complexion of "Arab-world-versus-the-rest" rather than investigates conflict between Arab states.[28] In addition, a regional dialogue between intellectuals has begun to emerge, especially on stations like al-Jazeera and in the pages of *al-Hayat*. To an important degree, this dialogue has expanded the bounds of debate in the Arab world, as it represents the injection of both new views and the back-and-forth of discussion into areas where such things had been relatively rare. This dialogue has also had the effect, however, of solidifying an "Arab consensus," which can become its own form of restraint. That is to say, as discussion is taken more seriously, serious dissent from widely held opinions becomes more precarious. Whereas many regimes protected the roles of "loyal oppositionists" in the past, the regional Arab marketplace may not be so kind to them in the future.

An additional and unexpected consequence of the new transnational media is the extent to which they introduce Arabic speakers to forms of Arabic speech to which they had not previously been exposed. Like many classical languages, a relatively wide gulf exists between formal, written Arabic and its vernacular, spoken form. Whereas formal Arabic is fairly uniform from place to place, spoken Arabic varies greatly, even within a single country. Some dialects are widely understood across the Arab world. More than a half century of Egyptian movies, radio broadcasts, and television serials (combined with a steady flow of Egyptian schoolteachers throughout the region) have ensured that Egyptian colloquial Arabic is the most widely understood in the Arab world. Other dialects, like Moroccan, are difficult even for native Arabic speakers from other countries to decipher. Satellite television has served as an important medium for introducing Arabs to unfamiliar dialects and breaking down some of the verbal barriers that divide the region. This process is still in a very early stage and homogenization of the language is still a long way off, but it is an important example of ways in which ties between Arabs have been strengthened by the new technology and barriers have been broken down.

The question (unanswered as of yet) is whether the growing sense of regional integration will be generally a force for dissension or one for accord. On the one hand, the new media are acting in many ways to integrate the Arab world with the West—not only by bringing the Western style of press inquiry to the region, with its concomitant effects on politics, but also in extending the reach of Western consumer culture and the icons of Western culture more broadly. One might reasonably expect that the diminution of differences between Arab and Western culture would promote mutual understanding, or at least expand the common ground on which Arabs and Westerners can interact. One could also envision, however, a situation in which the establishment of a "pan-Arab" culture unites Arabs at the expense of Arab–Western relations, strengthening already extant sentiments that the Arabs have suffered at Western hands, and increasing tensions between the two. Under a "Clash of Civilizations" scenario,[29] Western technology and political structures would coalesce around anti-Western themes, at the same time embracing the Western media but rejecting the Western message.

The "regionalization" of news has had an especially important influence on Arab public opinion toward the Arab–Israeli conflict. On the one hand, Arab television has blasted away the isolation experienced by Israeli politicians and policymakers. Israeli prime minister Binyamin Netanyahu appeared on an Orbit call-in show in 1996, for example, and a growing number of historical documentaries appearing on Arab television include interviews with relevant Israeli figures. No longer content to provide a one-sided perspective on either history or the recent past, Arab producers are finding that including Israeli views increases a show's credibility and viewer interest. Israel is no longer ignored or denied in the Arab media, but increasingly is presented as an important regional actor.

At the same time, transnational Arab media (particularly the satellite television stations) are projecting negative images of Israel to the region. Using a network of television reporters in Israel and the Palestinian autonomous areas, Arab stations regularly include in their evening broadcasts reports on Israeli settlement construction, home demolition, and open conflict with Palestinian Arabs. At the same time, the Arab media (print, television, and internet) closely monitor the statements of the Israeli government and often evince a rather sophisticated understanding of Israeli internal politics and Israeli governmental policy. Although there is no systematic evidence that the new media have contributed to a hardening of positions against Israel in the last few years, in conversations with a wide variety of Arab viewers the conclusion seems clear: The Arab media do appear to have an influence on public opinion, and when there is little good news to report on the Arab–Israeli front, that influence is anti-Israeli.

An interesting (but currently unanswerable) question is whether the Arab media could be helpful in ameliorating Arab–Israeli tensions if the climate were improving. On the one hand, the rise of communal feeling, which the regional media could be expected to promote, would advance Arab interests at the expense of non-Arab neighbors. On the other hand, confidence-building gestures could be communicated directly to the Arab public unmediated by Arab governments. On balance, it does not appear that there is anything inherent in the media to promote either rapprochement or conflict, either with Israel or with the West.

RISE OF A CHAOTIC INFORMATION REGIME

It has become a truism of Western writing about the Arab world to talk about the fatalism, lack of independent thinking, and subjection to authority that prevail in the region. Whether the supposed "failure" of Arab societies is attributed to characteristics of Islam, "hydraulic societies," or "Asiatic modes of production," there is a tendency for Europeans and Americans to see intellectual life in the Arab world as a dismal affair, at least for the last half-millennium.

Although this image is simplistic and exaggerated, there is a kernel of truth to it. Whereas Western societies have for centuries delegated a large degree of moral autonomy to the individual, such a phenomenon has not become widespread in the Arab world. That is to say, although it is normal (if inquisitive) to say to someone in the West, "What do you believe about God?" the normal question in the Arab world would be "What is your religion?" on the assumption that someone would adhere to orthodox religious beliefs even if one's observance diverged from orthodox practice.[30] There have certainly been innovative and free-thinking Arabs, as well as Westerners who submit blindly to authority, but it is probably accurate to say that individual reasoning (even in the absence of much knowledge) is a more highly prized characteristic in Europe and America than in the Arab world.

Changes underway suggest that this difference is likely to decrease over time. On the one hand, sharp advances in education and literacy are empowering individuals in a new way. As one scholar has suggested, what is new

> is the unprecedented access that ordinary people now have to sources of information and knowledge about religion and other aspects of their society. Quite simply, in country after country, government officials, traditional religious scholars, and officially sanctioned preachers are finding it very hard to monopolize the tools of literate culture.[31]

As the foregoing passage suggests, literacy's increased empowerment of the individual extends beyond the religious realm to affect social and political thinking as well. Current censorship battles, whether they involve the literary analysis of religious texts by the Egyptian scholar Nasr Hamid Abu Zayd, or the call for a widespread reinterpretation of Islamic law by the Syrian Muhammad Shahrur, are more a sign of boundaries being tested than they are of a new repression in the region.

Increased literacy is not the only engine in this process. In many ways, international travel on the elite level has played just as important a role. It is no accident that much of the new and independent thinking in the regional news media has been led by Arabs who have studied and lived overseas and who, in some cases, still do so. As will be discussed below, technological advances reintegrate individuals (and their thoughts and words) from the Arab diaspora into the Arab world. Undeniably, in country after country, the domestic media have absorbed more and more of the "internationalist" mode—they have become more challenging and more exciting, and, in all but a few countries, they have abandoned the practice of simply parroting a government "line" handed down from above. A close observer of Persian Gulf politics wrote in 1997:

> It seems to me that it is now much easier for more people in the Gulf to be exposed to views and interpretations of politics that are counter to those of their governments. These governments have never had a monopoly on "truth" for their societies, but now their challengers have broader audiences to which to appeal in writing, and more ways to get the written word into their hands and homes. Tolerance might not result, but this certainly "pluralizes" the market of ideas.[32]

As a consequence of this emerging marketplace of ideas, the currency of an idea increasingly depends not so much on its sponsor as it does the public's receptivity to it. Whereas public acclaim is not always a good indicator of an idea's worth, the emergence of a marketplace of ideas does serve to undermine unworthy ideas before they become longstanding policy.[33]

In addition, the rapid expansion of information available to Arabs will put an increased premium on their ability to sort through that information and separate the important and meaningful from the scurrilous or irrelevant. As two veteran political scientists explained in a recent journal article, "A plentitude of information leads to a poverty of attention . . . The low cost of transmitting data means that the ability to transmit it is much less important than it used to be, but the ability to filter information is more so. Political struggles focus less on control over the ability to transmit information than over the creation and destruction of credibility."[34] Credibility is the product of an active evaluative process by recipients of information. The ability to assess the credibility of information depends partly on experience and partly on trust, and it is a skill that can be learned and improved. In an Arab world awash in information of all kinds, individuals are called on to evaluate data countless times in a single day. Not all credibility assessments focus on political information; in the intermediate term, the bulk of them will probably involve commerce, as consumers evaluate the various brand-name products seeking to establish themselves in the Arab market.[35] The likely effect on politics is clear, however. With the rapid growth in the amount of information that reaches them, Arabs will have to evaluate political data and reports with a more critical eye than they have done to date, and governments will have to put forward information in a competitive marketplace of ideas in which those ideas will increasingly stand or fall based on their acceptability to the public rather than on governments' ability to compel their acceptance.

PUBLIC OPINION AND ARAB IDENTITY

The increased debate about public policy issues has resulted in many governments' increased need to be attentive to public opinion. Decreasingly satisfied with accepting government "lines," Arabs have increasingly engaged in domestic discussions throughout the region that have served to shape government opinion instead of merely being shaped by it. For example, in private discussions with U.S. government officials in late 1997 and early 1998, regional leaders frequently cited public opinion concerns to explain their reluctance publicly to support the use of force against Iraq, regardless of their distaste for Saddam Husayn. Public opinion is also cited by some Arab leaders as a powerful force in their calling for the normalization of relations between all Arab countries, which would involve rehabilitating Iraq, Libya, and even Sudan from their current positions as rogue states subject to international sanctions. Widescale efforts to aid the "suffering of the Iraqi people" have been increasingly visible in the Arab world, although in all cases the suffering has been described as a consequence of international sanctions, not the brutal dictatorship of Saddam Husayn.[36] The issue is not so much that these "rogue" regimes are honorable but that they are Arab. Many Arabs perceive that these countries have been singled out for opprobrium because of their Arabness, and for that reason all Arabs should rally around their cause. Another issue that has become ascendent in recent years is the idea of preserving an Arab Jerusalem. Arab television stations have telethons for their causes, and foundations establish sites on the worldwide web.

Interestingly, Islam has also emerged in some elements of the media as a unifying force for the region. It is impossible to say whether this is driven primarily by the fact that the overwhelming majority of Arabs are Muslims, or by the dominance of Saudi financing in the transnational Arab media. Nevertheless, it important to note that, whereas states and elites led the charge for pan-Arabism in the 1950s and 1960s, transnational Islamic movements and their mass followings are much more important actors today, and their efforts are being significantly abetted by the new media.

A final impetus for the "new Arabism" is that as Arabs interact with non-Arabs, they become increasingly aware of their "Arabness." Although none of this obviates their loyalties and identifications with their individual states, Arabs' increasing interaction with non-Arab cultures, and their treatment by those cultures as Arabs rather than as holders of specific nationalities, moves Egyptians, Syrians, Palestinians, and Saudi Arabians to have a heightened Arab identity vis-à-vis the outside world.

REINTEGRATION OF ARAB DIASPORAS

One of the most fascinating results of the new transnational media is the extent to which they have allowed the reintegration of Arab emigrants into Arab life and society. No longer cut off from their homelands, many Arabs living in the West read Arab newspapers (either in print or on the internet), watch Arab television (MBC, ART, and LBC are available in the United States by satellite and in some areas by cable), and actively seek out Arab sites on the internet. Even Iraq's United Nations ambassador, Nizar Hamdoon, breaks out of his isolation in New York by heavily using the internet. He told the *Washington Post*, "I do the internet, I keep up with the latest news, I browse through the CNN page and the web sites of newspapers I cannot get here . . . There are lots of Iraqi community chat rooms. I don't give my name. Regardless of their political social or economic background, they [the people in the online chat rooms] all feel that what is happening to the Iraqi people is unfair."[37]

The image is a startling one, but the fact is that there is an online community of Arabs based simultaneously in London, New York, and many cities of the region. As the amount of information about the Arab world available outside the Arab world blossoms, location becomes less and less relevant for one to play an active rule in modern Arab society.

Something as mundane as decreasing prices for international telephone calls play a role as well. For many years, countries have raised the price of or taxed international phone service to subsidize domestic operations. Under World Trade Organization rules, however, international phone tariffs are expected to drop precipitously in the coming years. As they plummet, so too will the costs of faxes and other transmissions of information over phone lines (including the use of international phone lines for internet access). Because of relative ease of use and a large installed base, in the intermediate term the telephone may prove more important than the internet as a conduit for new ideas to enter the Arab world and for reports of conditions within the Arab world to reach Arab communities outside.

The enlargement of the Arab community to bring Arabs back into contact with their own societies (and doing so increasingly through interactive media, given the growing prevalence of the internet in the United States) has had the remarkable effect of reinserting expatriate Arab intellectuals into the Arab world. A host of Western-based Arab academics—many of whom left the Middle East to undertake doctoral research and then found employment in the West studying the Arab world—are becoming fixtures in the new Arab media.[38] Western-based Arab newspaper correspondents and columnists also "write back" into the Arab world, and they are clearly affected by their surroundings. The internationalization of media coverage has, to a great degree, become like a huge exchange program, in some ways making the West more aware of Arab concerns, but in many ways making the Arab world more aware of the political and social mores of the West. There is a remarkable cross-fertilization of ideas taking place between Arab intellectuals in the West and their colleagues remaining in the Arab world, enabled and driven by the new media.

Even within overseas Arab communities, the internet is causing fascinating changes. As anthropologist Jon Anderson points out, online "communities"—chat rooms, bulletin boards, usenet groups, and so forth—are not typical of the societies from which their members have emerged. The online Arab community is disproportionately composed of scientists, engineers, and students; theologians, politicians, and military officials are underrepresented. The result, Anderson reports, is that individuals who at home would yield to the opinions of specialists find themselves venturing into religious and political topics. In so doing they bring the insights and tools of their professional training to the discussion, resulting in a new "creole" discourse that combines elements of discourse from their own places of origin with Western scientific training and scholarly inquiry.[39] Arabs still in the Arab world can monitor and participate in most if not all of these discussions, although in doing so they are potentially subject to the same sorts of monitoring that characterize all of their internet use.

In all of this cross-fertilization, there are two groups involved. The first are bilingual Arabs, resident either in the West or in the Arab world. They have a choice of language in which to communicate, and often they will communicate some kinds of messages in Arabic and others in Western languages, especially English. The second group, however, consists of a larger group of Arabs who are not bilingual. For this group, the media are considerably more important and more broadening. The transnational Arab media become not only their link to other Arabs, but also a fundamental link to the rest of the world. Although some dismiss the new ideas as "corrupting," for large portions of the Arab public this link to the rest of the world is both fascinating and desirable.

There remain large segments of the population, however, for which the changes outlined above are irrelevant to their lives. The regional Arab media remain something of a rich man's game, and penetration beyond the elite level is slight except in wealthy Gulf states. The effects of the "cross-fertilization" of ideas and reintegration of diasporas will be uneven in the short and intermediate term, although the strong desire for transnational media among the elites in country after country suggest that the media will have a strong effect, even if that effect is from the top down.

THE GROWING IMPORTANCE OF MARKET FORCES

To date, market forces have played a relatively minor role in Arab countries. State sectors have generally been strong (either as a legacy of Arab socialism or as a consequence of state control over petroleum revenues), and private sectors have been somewhat weak. States have either owned media outlets outright or orchestrated the existence or demise of those outlets. Advertising revenues—the mother's milk of media production the world over—has been paltry. As former *al-Hayat* editor Jihad al-Khazen bemoaned, total advertising spending in the Arab world in 1994 was $900 million, while Israel itself had an advertising expenditure of $800 million.[40]

Yet, the trend has begun to shift. The regional Arabic-language print and satellite-broadcast media described above have seen a marked increase in advertising spending in recent years. In 1997 alone, for example, advertising spending on pan-Arab (i.e., satellite) television grew by 96 percent over the previous year, to $202 million.[41] Between 1995 and 1997, advertising spending in pan-Arab magazines increased by 36 percent, and in newspapers by 14 percent.[42] The total Arab advertising market has enlarged as well, growing from $1.13 billion in 1995 to $1.54 billion in 1997.

The products advertised are familiar to most Americans. The top ten brands advertised in the regional Arab media and in the member states of the Gulf Cooperation Council (GCC) are Toyota, Nissan, Marlboro, BMW, Pampers, Pantene, Hyundai, Ford, and Chevrolet.[43] Pampers is the most advertised brand on television in this market, followed by Pantene. Toyota leads in newspaper spending, and Marlboro in magazines. By type of product, the most advertised products on pan-Arab television were adult personal hygiene and health products, followed by shampoos and other hair products, and candy and snacks.[44] The foregoing suggests that what is emerging is not merely a Western-style advertising market, but Western-style brand-name development, Western-style consumption patterns, and personal lifestyles that are more Western, at least in their outward manifestations.

This trend toward Westernization is neither a completed process nor a foregone conclusion; in addition, it is hard to foresee how more Western consumption patterns (disposable or consumable branded goods) might affect other aspects of Arab life. It has become a trope of Western media reports about Saudi Arabia and Iran to note that veiled women in those countries are sometimes impeccably dressed under their black cloaks, but whether such patterns of dressing (and consumption) reflect a stable situation or one on the verge of change remains unclear.

What is clear, however, is that the shape of the Arab media in the future very much depends on the shape of the Arab media market, and that market is dependent on a continued shift toward higher per capita incomes and increasingly Western patterns of consumption. If the media market grows, media outlets will continue to experiment with content to draw more viewers. Arab viewers will likely see more sex and scandal, and political coverage will likely grow more daring, at least in the near and intermediate term (but they will undoubtedly continue to shy away from offending Saudi political sensibilities). Although in the future not all television may resemble LBC or al-Jazeera, the two stations have proved that Arabs thirst for new kinds of programming; meanwhile, the continued high viewership of MBC suggests that even playing things relatively straight can create a powerful media force in the region.

The important thing to keep in mind is that if the media in the Middle East become more market-oriented, they will provide more of what people want to see and read. This will not necessarily be highbrow material, but if the Western experience is any guide, the Arab media will find that pushing boundaries often proves a more successful strategy than staying far away from them.[45] In such a scenario, a more market-oriented Arab media could be expected to be more daring on sex and politics than what has been the case, although one would expect that they would retain some respect for regional mores, at least in the intermediate term. If the broadcasts and printed press are too "out there," they merely come across as imports, and that can affect their broad acceptance.

That marketing expenses will rise enough to make broadcasting profitable (or at least to keep losses to an acceptable level) is by no means certain. Persistently low prices for petroleum products will depress the economies not only of the Gulf states, but also of the countries that export labor to those states. Lack of a marketing infrastructure discourages advertising as well. The difficulty this author had in determining even broad ranges of viewerships for leading television programs—and the corresponding difficulty marketers must have in determining who is seeing their advertising and buying their products—is a barrier to increasing advertising expenditures enough to sustain a broad mix of television programming.

In the event that free-to-air stations never become commercially viable, the satellite television market will likely become bifurcated. The first resulting segment would be state-sponsored satellite television. While Qatari-backed al-Jazeera has challenged the status quo, with time and the intervention of governmental interests it seems more likely that the future face of government-sponsored television will be more staid. There will be a strong impetus for states to essentially sign nonaggression pacts regarding their state-run media, and the media will again emerge as the foreign policy tool that they were when Gamal Abdel Nasser first harnessed them in the 1950s and 1960s. Whereas many satellite stations are now based out of Europe, their migration back to the region and increasing government control over their operations will tend to dampen their aggressive news coverage.

The other part of the market likely to survive would comprise the fee-for-service stations like ART and Orbit, driven by high per-user fees and a superior ability to monitor the viewing habits of their wealthy customers. How many such networks the market can sustain and at what level of fees is unclear, but they appear to have identified a way to remain afloat without subsidies from outside parties. For the foreseeable future, these stations seem destined to have their sights fixed mostly on the Saudi market, where incomes are highest (and individuals are most able to pay the requisite fees) and entertainment alternatives the lowest. Whether viewers of such stations will, under the influence of Western-oriented programming, become so unlike their countrymen in dress and speech as to pose a social or political problem for their societies is unclear. Clearly, factors other than television are influencing Arab behavior; still, the January 1997 arrest of seventy-six young adults in Egypt—many of them students at the American University in Cairo—for "satanic practices" influenced by their watching American music videos on satellite television must be a cautionary tale. In many poorer societies in the Arab world, satellite television is contributing to a phenomenon in which some segments of society are educated and oriented in an entirely different way than the mass of their compatriots.[46]

MIGRATION OF PRODUCTION BACK TO THE REGION

An additional result of the increasing market orientation of the Arab media is their likely migration back to the region for at least some of their production. Producing material in high-cost cities like London, New York, and Washington cannot compete economically with the production costs in Amman, Cairo, or possibly Beirut. Of course, many of the regional Arab media have been shaped by their growth outside the Arab world and are more liberal in their approach to social and political affairs than was common heretofore in Arab countries; extraregional production allows them a somewhat greater degree of freedom of expression. Yet, the time will come, sooner rather than later, when economics will induce these organizations to return to the region. Their move will be eased by the generally more open media environment prevailing in the Arab world, especially in the cities mentioned above. Saudi-run organizations will have the most difficult choice to make, however, because the kingdom is among the least open societies in the region, and the efficiencies of doing business there are among the least compelling. Observers may therefore see Saudi-owned companies setting up shop in other Arab countries. ART has already done so with its move to Cairo; *al-Hayat* maintains a large operation in Cairo and may move the production of some of its pages to Beirut.

The still-nascent Arabic-language internet market lends itself to the off-shore basing of operations. Flourishing Jordanian- and Egyptian-based internet consultancies are a sign of how cost-effective it is to design products in one country and sell them in a second, more expensive country. The paying country need not even have an internet link of its own. The government of Iraq maintains web pages in Jordan, and Saudi companies can easily base their web page operations anywhere they wish (even the United States). All of the new media make the location of production secondary to the content of the product itself, and talented editors, writers, announcers, and programmers can work virtually anywhere.

THE INTERNET AND NEW TECHNOLOGIES

Much of the hype surrounding the spread of the internet in the United States and Europe has stressed the liberating aspects of access to information. A strong current, however, warns of the risks that the internet poses to privacy. Those risks are somewhat higher in the Arab world than they are in the United States, for two primary reasons.

On the one hand, Arab countries generally lack the privacy laws common in the United States, where such laws are predicated on the Fourth Amendment's protections against unreasonable search and seizure. Arab governments have generally had strong internal intelligence operations in the last half century, and limitations on governmental power in surveillance matters are rare indeed. Casual users of the internet can open themselves up to even greater monitoring than is already the case, and—absent privacy laws—such monitoring is more a likelihood than a mere possibility. Monitoring of internet use can include searching electronic mail (e-mail)—either in transit or stored in individual accounts—for key words, as well as keeping records of individual web sites visited by a user.[47] Such monitoring is relatively simple and inexpensive, and it is easier to cast a broad net using computer-generated searches than it is, for instance, to randomly tap telephone lines in the hope that a conversation is of interest to internal security forces.

The second factor allowing governments to monitor and control internet access is the generally small number of approved internet providers in any individual Arab country, and the small number of gateways (often only one) for all international internet traffic. Under such a structure, it is very difficult for internet activity to escape government purview. Without governmental restraint and controls on such monitoring, ordinary individuals will likely be subject to more monitoring than is presently the case.

Whereas ordinary citizens generally subject themselves to increased governmental surveillance by using the new technologies, sophisticated individuals may use the technology to gain more privacy in their communications, especially outgoing ones. E-mail messages can be sent easily via anonymous remailers, which strip the sender's identity from the message. Internet cafes that rent computer time allow a degree of anonymity as well. Finally, computer encryption programs are widely available and easy to use, and they are extremely difficult to decode.

On the one hand, such encryption provides political opposition groups, human rights monitors, and those merely seeking privacy with far greater freedom than they currently enjoy. But encryption also creates a serious law enforcement problem. A senior U.S. government official recently lamented privately that intercepted electronic communications are among the most valuable intelligence information he receives, and he expects the amount of such information available a decade from now will be only half of what he has today, because of encryption. Encrypted computer messages can be used to transmit personal or financial information, but they can also be used to plan terrorist attacks, incite violence, or transfer illicit funds. U.S. government decryption abilities are closely guarded secrets, but continued sparring between the government and the software industry over encryption standards suggest that Washington is worried. Currently, the U.S. government restricts the export of strong encryption software, but the ease of transporting software (physically or electronically) suggests that such software is likely making its way around the world. Arab governments' decryption abilities are significantly less robust than American abilities, and it is unclear how well they will cope with the criminal exchange of encrypted information.

Another communications option for escaping government monitoring may be new satellite-based mobile telephone networks that avoid national, land-based communications systems. As phone lines can be used to transmit voice, fax, or internet data, the new satellite phone networks may offer significant, if expensive, opportunities for secure communications in the coming decades. Human rights organizations and political opposition groups can rightly be cheered that technology has improved their ability to report on problematic conditions in an individual country, but the technology does not necessarily help them change those conditions (other than by providing more current and compelling incriminating evidence).

SUMMARY

Whereas some of the societal changes described above are not certain to take place, change brought on by new technology does seem certain. As increasing amounts of data flow faster and at lower costs, Arab governments will be hard-pressed to act in the "gatekeeper" role to which they have become accustomed. Poorly performing Arab economies will make the new technology relatively more expensive and uncommon in the short term, but the long-term results appear certain: increasing amounts of information, new ways of interpreting that information, and the rise of new kinds of communities predicated on common language and interests instead of geographic proximity.

NOTES

1   See *Routine Abuse, Routine Denial: Civil Rights and the Political Crisis in Bahrain* (Washington: Human Rights Watch, 1997), pp. 76–79.

2   Article 40 (b) of Amiri Decree 14/1979, published in issue 1344 of the *Official Gazette.* Ibid., p. 76.

3   The boundaries for discussion of Islamic issues vary from country to country, and they are significantly narrower in a country like Saudi Arabia, the government of which defines its authority as emanating in part from its role as a custodian of religious authenticity. Under such conditions, any discussion of religious views contrary to official pronouncements is suspect.

4   In a disturbing departure from practice, the government of Egypt appeared to respond languorously when Egyptian literary scholar Nasr Hamid Abu Zayd was charged with apostasy for arguing that Islamic religious texts partly reflect the age in which they were written rather than exist as an eternal truth for all time. Abu Zayd left Egypt and is now teaching in the Hague.

5   "New Press Law Goes into Effect," Arabic Media Internet Network, online at www.amin.org/En/eyeamn/9809/02/free01.htm.

6   "Jordan Bans London-Based *al-Quds al-Arabi*," Agence France Presse (AFP), May 12, 1998.

7   Alia Shukri Hamzeh, "Lawzi: Al Quds Al Arabi Ban Not Final," *Jordan Times* internet edition, May 18, 1998.

8   Ibid.

9   "Jordan Bans London-Based *al-Quds al-Arabi*," AFP.

10 Wireless cable broadcasts or rebroadcasts over terrestrial channels can, of course, be censored by the government, which may explain some of their appeal to regional authorities.

11 Marwan al-Khatib, "The Internet: Will the Arabs Lose the Battle of the Future?" *al-Wasat* (in Arabic), July 6–12, 1998, p. 34. The "Indonesia" comment refers to the broad popular uprising in the summer of 1998 that deposed Indonesian president Suharto after thirty years of strong-man rule.

12 See *al-Sabil* report, May 5–11, 1997, p. 1, translated as "Jordan TV Bans Reports on Anti-US Protests, Layth Shubaylat," in FBIS-NES-98-125 (Foreign Broadcast Information Service–Near East and South Asia, Daily Report online), May 5, 1998.

13 Howard Kurtz, *Spin Cycle* (New York: Free Press, 1998).

14 Abdel Bari Atwan, "Kingdom of Censorship," undated manuscript given to the author.

15 Abdel Bari Atwan and Jihad Khazen, "In the Saudi Pocket," *Index on Censorship* 2 (1996), p. 51.

16 It is worth noting that criticism is both visible on the Qatari-owned al-Jazeera satellite channel and abundantly available over the internet.

17 The incident is reported, among other places, in UN Economic and Social Council Document E/CN.4/1995/34 (January 12, 1995).

18 Atwan and Khazen, "In the Saudi Pocket," p. 53.

19 Ibid., p. 52.

20 See, for example, Walter Armbrust, "Egyptian Cinema Challenged by Global, Regional Changes," *CCAS News* (a newsletter published by the Georgetown Center for Contemporary Arab Studies), December 1997, p. 1.

21 On May 17, 1998, the Moroccan Ministry of Communications blasted al-Jazeera for planning to broadcast an interview with a spokesman for the Polisario Front, which seeks the independence of the Western Sahara from Moroccan control. Moroccans rejected the offer to provide a rebuttal to the Polisario spokesman, arguing that doing so would equate "the Moroccan people with a group of mercenaries working for foreign purposes." The interview aired anyway. See "Morocco Slams Doha-based TV on Western Sahara," Reuters, May 17, 1998.

22 Many states, like Kuwait, choose to maintain a great deal of domestic press freedom, but that freedom can be eroded by government decree.

23 Presentation by Prof. Andrea Kavanaugh, Georgetown University, February 13, 1998.

24 The Tunisian decree on encrypted e-mail messages is "Arrêté du ministre des communications du 9 septembre 1997 fixant les conditions d'utilisation du cryptage dans l'exploitation des services à valeur ajoutée des télécommunications." I am grateful to Eric Goldstein of Human Rights Watch for bringing this document to my attention.

25 The transmission of encrypted messages over the internet can pose a serious security threat to governments. According to one source, Israeli Shin Bet investigators claimed that terrorists in Britain were sending "a full range of instructions for terrorist attack" via encrypted messages over the internet, "including maps, photographs, directions, codes, and even technical details of how to use bombs." The technical requirements to send such encrypted

THE WASHINGTON INSTITUTE FOR NEAR EAST POLICY

messages are relatively modest, and the ability of governments to penetrate them are rather meager. According to one Israeli expert, "In order to stop this transfer of information, we would have to cut all telephone lines for international calls." *Foreign Report,* September 25, 1997.

26 It is perhaps worth noting that U.S. government security regulations permit documents classified up to "Secret" to be sent through the U.S. mail as long as they are sent in unmarked white envelopes. The presumption is that there are so many similar envelopes in the mail flow that finding the one with a sensitive message would be like finding a needle in a haystack. The global flow of electronic information increasingly resembles that haystack.

27 Benedict Anderson, *Imagined Communities: Reflections on the Origin and Spread of Nationalism*, 2nd ed. (London: Verso, 1991), pp. 44–45.

28 On the subject of the changing "complexion" of Arab reportage, see for example, Shibley Telhami in Jon B. Alterman, ed., *Sadat and His Legacy: Egypt and the World, 1977–1997* (Washington: The Washington Institute for Near East Policy, 1998), pp. 98–99.

29 The "Clash of Civilizations" scenario is named after the seminal article of the same name by Samuel Huntington, *Foreign Affairs* 72, no. 3 (Summer 1993), pp. 22–49.

30 The author's favorite anecdote concerning Arab attitudes toward the moral autonomy of the individual is the comment of an Egyptian acquaintance, probably illiterate, who asked if it were true that there were people in America who do not believe in God. Upon learning the affirmative he asked, "What do you do to them?" "Nothing." "You mean you just let them walk in the street?"

31 Dale F. Eickelman, "Inside the Islamic Reformation," *Wilson Quarterly* (Winter 1998), p. 82.

32 F. Gregory Gause III, "Political Opposition in the Gulf Monarchies," unpublished conference paper, delivered at "The Changing Security Agenda in the Gulf," Doha, Qatar, October 24–26, 1997.

33 The role of a marketplace in helping to determine a product or theory's worth can also be applied to public-sector industries, which are distinguished not by the fact that all were failures but rather by the fact that the ones that were failures were allowed to persist indefinitely because governments had no profit motive to shut them down.

34 Robert Keohane and Joseph Nye, Jr., "States and the Information Revolution," *Foreign Affairs* (September/October 1998), p. 89–90.

35 Brand identity in large part consists of establishing credibility for the consistent performance characteristics of a specific product or family of products.

36 Anyone not familiar with just how brutal the Iraqi regime is would do well to read Samir al-Khalil, *Republic of Fear: The Politics of Modern Iraq (London: Hutchinson, 1989).*

37 Nora Boustany, "The Loneliest Diplomat," *Washington Post*, February 18, 1998, p. 17.

38 Examples of Arab academics living in the West but increasingly rejoining the Arab world by way of the new media include but are in no way limited to Professors Clovis Maksoud, Shibley Telhami, and Ibrahim Karawan.

39 Jon W. Anderson, "Middle East Diasporas on the Internet,"conference paper, online at linus.isoc.org/inet96/proceedings/e8/e8_2.htm.

40 Jihad Khazen in Abdel Bari Atwan and Jihad Khazen, "In the Saudi Pocket," *Index on Censorship 2* (1996), p. 52.

41 Pan-Arab Research Center, "1997 Arab World Advertising Harvest: Ladders and Snakes on the Growth Track, But Slower than Forecasted."

42 Advertising expenditures in pan-Arab magazines rose to $83 million, and in pan-Arab newspapers to $12 million. It is worth noting that in every individual Arab country, spending on newspaper advertising dwarfed that spent on magazines, but in the pan-Arab market, spending on magazine advertising is about six times the level of spending on newspaper advertising. Ibid.

43 Both Pampers and Pantene are brands owned by American consumer giant Procter and Gamble.

44 Ibid.

45 Even if the Arab media become more market-oriented, this is not to say that they will necessarily evolve into a responsible social or political force. In a widely publicized speech at Cornell University in May 1998, MSNBC host Keith Olbermann began by saying, "I work in television, an industry in which the total number of moral choices may, this year, actually exceed last year's total, which I believe was 19 correct moral decisions, out of 975,365,272 opportunities." Keith Olbermann, "Blame Me, Too," *Brill's Content*, September 1998, p. 90.

46 The father of one of the arrested Egyptian students complained to the Cairo magazine *Ruz al-Yusef*, "There is an incapacity among (police) officials to read the facts. They are acting as if they are unaware that this music which they call incriminating is broadcast 24 hours daily on satellite TV." John Daniszewski, *Calgary Herald*, February 15, 1997, p. C3.

47 Web sites can be barred by access providers, but this is more of a freedom of expression concern than a privacy one.

Chapter 6

Conclusions and Policy Recommendations

T he transnational media in the Arab world appear destined to grow in the future, particularly because they are technology-driven. Just as the sudden availability of cheap transistor radios in the 1960s created new opportunities for transmitting political ideas across borders, advances in the speedy and inexpensive dissemination of data are the engine behind current changes. Unlike the 1960s, however, the new transnational media are not avowedly political. Whereas Gamal Abdel Nasser's *Voice of the Arabs* programming sought to undermine the political status quo in the region and to advance Egypt's foreign policy agenda, today's Arab newspapers, satellite broadcasts, and internet communications are created by multinational staffs, and they are generally (but not entirely) driven by the pursuit of commercial profits.

PRIVATE VERSUS STATE CONTROL

The key factor that will shape these transnational media in the future will be the long-term commercial viability of the enterprises. At the present time, all of the major international Arabic newspapers and most of the major satellite stations are privately owned. If the transnational Arab media prove to be commercially viable, their content will be primarily (though certainly not entirely) guided by the interests of their readership and viewership. As in the West, they will likely contain information that is in some way provocative or exciting, in the pursuit of market share. Competition among a broad array of outlets will ensure that there will be few

73

sacred cows, and the political and social repercussions will likely be felt throughout the region.

Even if private financing proves commercially viable, however, Saudi Arabia will probably continue to escape serious criticism, at least via the capital-intensive print and satellite television media.[1] Saudi pockets are among the deepest in the region, and Saudi capitalists own the media companies that produce the content, own the businesses whose advertising supports the content, and constitute the consumers who are most attractive to advertisers. More narrowly, Saudi Arabia has a large number of individuals who are allied with the state but do not hold official posts. Members of the royal family, like super-investor Prince al-Walid bin Talal; royal relations, like MBC-owner Shaykh Walid al-Ibrahim; and leading merchants, like ART-owner Shaykh Salah Kamel, exist in symbiotic relation to the state without explicitly being a part of it. On the one hand, their informal relationships with the state enrich them, but on the other, their relationships also ensure these Saudis' loyalty to the interests of the kingdom. Such individuals are able to ensure that the regional media are sensitive to the Saudi rulers' concerns on issues of key interest to the state. In so doing, they bar almost any discussion of Saudi internal developments or opposition to the Saudi monarchy. Such rules are never stated, but they are widely understood among those working in the regional Arab media, and they are likely to persist.

It is possible that the regional Arabic media will be unable to prove financially viable in the intermediate term.[2] Continued low oil prices, low levels of intraregional trade, and sluggish economic growth may all combine to undermine the move toward an independent media market in the Arab world. In that event, states may seek to step in and take the place of private broadcasters. Qatar already controls one of the most widely watched satellite channels (al-Jazeera); Egypt and Dubai have active regional broadcasting programs; and countries from Libya to Yemen to Iraq are seeking to broadcast their programming over satellites as well. A state-led media market could be expected to be more respectful of regional powers than would a commercially led market, and states would likely pursue the sorts of "nonaggression pacts" in news coverage that are already reportedly in place among many countries. Cooperation between Arab states has been notoriously difficult to implement, however, and despite rhetorical deference to the idea of cooperation, in practice there have been few durable regional agreements in the last half century. Even if comprehensive regional media protocols could be created, disputes would inevitably occur, national media outlets would defect from regional agreements, and residents of the various countries in the region will find it far easier than ever before to get exposure to new ideas regardless of the efforts or desires of their individual governments.

Such agreements would be more effective if they were to seek to limit information of a more cultural nature, such as gender relations or modes of dress. Countries do not have a vital stake in such issues, and absent a commercial motive to do otherwise, the incentives for compliance with regional norms may prove powerful. Even so, countries like Lebanon and Egypt fiercely resist efforts to impose Persian Gulf norms on their more open societies, and the long term efficacy of any such agreements is far from clear.

THE INTERNET AND CENSORSHIP

Although ardent enthusiasts point to the internet as an antidote to state power in the Arab world, thus far their enthusiasm is misplaced. Internet penetration remains small, and more important, the internet is subject to blocking and monitoring. With an ability to search stored messages and internet traffic for key words or specific strings of characters, governments can monitor the internet even more efficiently and effectively than they can other media.

Yet, government efforts to do so face stiff challenges from a more sophisticated base of users who use anonymous remailers, public terminals, encryption software, or a combination of all three. Whereas the internet empowers human rights monitors and opposition political movements, it also empowers terrorists and criminals by offering new, fast means of communication and by making their activities more difficult to monitor.

The internet, as well as satellite-based telephone services beyond the control of individual nations, primarily give security to personal communications between individuals and are less effective in reaching mass audiences. The likely long-term result, however, will be the decline of censorship throughout the region. Although this decline will be halting and uneven at times, regimes will find themselves hard-pressed to contain and control information from a rapidly growing number of outlets sending more information more easily and inexpensively than ever before. Governments that attempt to restrain or block information will find themselves at a relative disadvantage when trying to attract investment in the global marketplace, and businesses in such countries will suffer from burdens not imposed on their competitors. The sheer expense of establishing an apparatus to monitor the vast quantity of information making its way around the world—only to have that apparatus be ineffective—will be another disincentive to government censorship.

In the near and intermediate term, Arab governments will likely try to establish themselves as intermediaries between their citizens and information. Wireless cable television systems and government-based internet systems will grow in the coming years as part of such an effort. But as increasing amounts of information in the world are targeted at increasingly narrow audiences, Arab governments may well find that efforts to insulate their societies from foreign ideas is a Sisyphean task. The volume and variety of information passing back and forth will overwhelm any apparatus established to restrain that information.

In the last few years, many Arabs have seen an alarming increase in censorship activities by governments, most commonly directed against print journalists. Rather than presage the future of Arab journalism, however, increased efforts at censorship more likely represent government responses to a new media environment that the governments can only imperfectly shape. Because they cannot control satellite broadcasts or the still-nascent internet, governments have retreated into taking the kinds of actions they know how to take from years of print censorship. In the new media environment, however, such moves are generally ineffective, and they can be expected to diminish in the coming years.

THE RETURN OF 'ARABISM'

An important long-term effect of the new Arab media is the return of a sense of "Arabism" to the region after a decline of several decades. In fact, the "new Arabism" is led by publics rather than states (which led the old version) and is quite different from what has come before. The "new Arabism" tends to be Islamic-leaning rather than secular, and it emanates from the Persian Gulf region rather than the Levant. Like the old Arabism, it has linguistic and historical roots, but it creates a sense of immediacy and an unmediated community that were impossible without the new technologies. The greater exchange of ideas through the region and a concomitant increased strength of transnational movements in the region is not only possible but likely.

It is important to recall, however, that this regional dialogue will engage only a small percentage of the Arab public, particularly in poorer Arab countries, where few can afford access to the new media and only a portion of those few also care about regional political issues. In some individual states, then, the political effect may be disruptive as a regionally oriented bourgeoisie clashes with more nationalistically oriented groups in their own countries.

An emergent "new Arabism" could pose significant challenges for U.S. interests in the Middle East, especially if anti-Americanism becomes a central component of that movement. Opinion pages of Arab newspapers and guests on Arab television shows increasingly accuse the United States of maintaining different rules for Muslim and non-Muslim countries, imposing draconian punishments on the former while overlooking the transgressions of the latter. Unilateral American action in the region—from the Arab–Israeli arena to the dual containment of Iraq and Iran—may appear necessary to U.S. policymakers, but it also makes the United States loom as a large target for the hostile and disaffected.

Recent American efforts to distinguish between Islam and the actions of some Muslims, including presidential holiday greetings, Muslim celebrations in the White House, and explicitly distinguishing between Islam and the actions of Islamist terrorists, may have gone some way toward assuaging Arab feelings. At the same time, however, new technologies have empowered groups with anti-American messages to convey those messages regardless of the wishes of pro-American governments in the region. By its nature, the new Arabism need not be inimical to U.S. interests, but it certainly may turn out to be. In the recent past, Arabism has often expressed itself in terms of what it is not: anti-Western, anti-American, anti-Israeli. A more conservative version of the new Arabism, which focuses on social advancement, increased regional trade, regional cooperation against terrorism, diminishing interstate tensions, and supporting common efforts against regional threats like rogue actors and weapons of mass destruction, may not only improve conditions in the Arab world but would also serve U.S. interests.

POLICY RECOMMENDATIONS

- *Engage the emerging class of internationally attuned Arabs.* The transnational media are in some ways aiding and in some ways reflecting the rise of a new bourgeoisie in the Arab world, one that is generally well-educated and well-traveled. The Arabs of this class who came of age in the 1960s and 1970s are familiar with the shortcomings of their parents' generation. Although these younger Arabs are not ideologically united, they share a cosmopolitan viewpoint. As opinion leaders in their own societies and in the Arab world at large, they will play a major role in shaping their countries' attitudes toward the West and Western interests in the region and around the world. This group has created the new regional Arab media, and it is among the new media's most avid consumers.

- *Win support among monolingual middle classes.* Whereas most of the individuals active in creating the new regional Arab media are bilingual, many consumers of the regional Arab media are monolingual. By paying attention to the regional Arabic media, these individuals manifest an interest in world affairs and are open to different viewpoints. Although individuals in this "second stratum" are rarely opinion-shapers on the national level, they represent an important link between the elites and the broad public and can play a crucial role in determining the future directions of Arab societies.

- *Better understand the changing nature of public opinion in the Arab world.* As Western-style education spreads among Arabs and news sources become more diverse, Arab governments will find it increasingly difficult to steer public opinion. The pan-Arab media have already proved a powerful force in stirring up anger against United Nations sanctions on Iraq, as well as against the slow pace of Israeli–Palestinian peace negotiations. Although individual leaders may desire closer ties to the West, to Israel, or to other regional states (or, contrarily, they may prefer more adversarial ties), they will have an increasingly difficult time molding public opinion, even if their abilities to shape the broad outlines of that opinion remain intact.

- *Encourage public diplomacy.* Whereas U.S. government officials for the last two decades have understood the importance of visual images in shaping public attitudes in the United States, they have been slow to understand the importance of those same images overseas. Since the beginning of this decade, satellite television has emerged as the dominant regional medium in the Arab world, and its viewership is rapidly expanding. There will likely always be a role for newspapers and magazines, especially for intellectual debate, and the internet may yet find its niche in the Arab world, although its presence is currently small.

Neither medium should be neglected as a channel for communication. For now, however, there is an urgent need to devise a communications strategy with the Arab world that acknowledges the importance of television images and that actively promotes U.S. policy through a medium which itself is largely American-created.

At the present time, no U.S. government officials appear on satellite television broadcasts in Arabic, and Arab reporters in Washington complain that it is often difficult to gain interviews in English with decision makers who deal with the Middle East. For the United States to have an effective public diplomacy strategy in the Arab world, these conditions must change.

To be sure, there has been progress in recent years. Officials appear to have conducted more background briefings for regional journalists, and the U.S. Information Agency has established a presence on the worldwide web in Arabic. Whereas such efforts are important, they are not sufficient. They do not produce compelling television images, and in the next decade, it will be compelling television images that matter.

If Americans want to influence the political thinking of the Arab world, they will have to do what Arab governments must: work with the transnational Arab media. The growing Arab media are emerging as increasingly reliable and important carriers of news and information, and the trend is likely to continue. The Arab media are generally beyond the control of individual governments, and they have manifested an interest in covering all points of view. At a time when the U.S. government's standing in the region is at low ebb, a concerted and sophisticated effort to engage the regional Arab media, and through them the Arab world at large, could reap great rewards. The media world is, after all, one that the United States had a large role in creating and which the U.S. government understands well. Success in this field could vastly facilitate the execution of U.S. policy in the region. Adherence to old modes of courting leaders and ignoring their publics could, in the early years of the next century, mean courting disappointment if not disaster.

NOTES

1   The internet allows virtually anyone to broadcast a message at low cost. Information from virulent opponents of the Saudi regime can be found at

web sites operated by the Committee for Defense of Legitimate Rights (www.umma.net/cdlr/) and its offshoot, the Movement for Islamic Reform in Arabia (www.miraserve.com).

2   Being financially viable does not necessarily mean turning a profit. There are a large number of money-losing publications in the United States. Most notably, the Unification Church has reportedly given the *Washington Times* more than $1 billion in subsidies. Other publications, including the *New Republic* and the *New Yorker*, also reportedly require outside funds to operate.

Recent Books
from The Washington Institute

IRAN UNDER KHATAMI
A Political, Economic, and Military Assessment
Patrick Clawson, Michael Eisenstadt,
Eliyahu Kanovsky, David Menashri

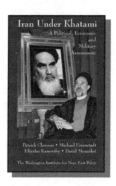

In an update of the Institute's best-selling Focus on Iran series, the authors analyze the changes in Iranian government policies in the year since Muhammad Khatami became president. Each chapter updates the author's previous book to create a comprehensive view of Iran's military, economy, and domestic politics. Includes an additional analysis of U.S. policies toward Iran, focusing on if—and how—these policies should change. *October 1998, 112 pp., ISBN 0-944029-27-2*

BUILDING TOWARD CRISIS
Saddam Husayn's Strategy for Survival
Amatzia Baram

U.S. Institute of Peace Scholar Amatzia Baram examines the domestic coalition supporting Saddam Husayn and techniques the Iraqi president uses to maintain that coalition. While providing an extensive look at Saddam's family tree and the importance of relations in understanding Saddam's power base, this book explains how the Iraqi president has used the international community to influence his domestic standing and to garner needed support in the Arab world. *Policy Paper no. 47, July 1998, 156 pp., ISBN 0-944029-25-6*

IRAQ STRATEGY REVIEW
Options for U.S. Policy
Patrick L. Clawson, editor

Seven years after the Gulf War, Saddam Husayn is still in power in Baghdad and still a thorn in America's side. Meanwhile, U.S. policy toward Iraq is under fire from critics both foreign and domestic. By presenting essays by six Middle East scholars that assess Washington's potential courses of action, *Iraq Strategy Review* offers a means of analyzing America's options regarding the Iraqi dictator. This book is an invaluable tool for U.S policymakers and others interested in America's Iraq policy. It provides the crucial starting point for public debate over how the United States should handle Saddam's Iraq. *July 1998, 180 pp., ISBN 0-944029-26-4*

'KNIVES, TANKS, AND MISSILES'
Israel's Security Revolution
Eliot Cohen, Michael Eisenstadt, Andrew Bacevich

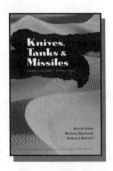

While the day's headlines focus on the stalemate in the Arab–Israeli peace process, the necessity of deterring and—potentially—fighting war remains the supreme challenge for Israel's leaders. Complicating this effort is the remarkable pace of technological change that has created what experts term a "revolution in military affairs." Weapons are "smarter" and more lethal than ever before, terrorism can now pose a strategic threat, and missiles can now bring an enemy thousands of miles away to a nation's borders. To understand the answers Israeli military planners and strategic thinkers have given to these critical questions—so as to glean appropriate lessons for the U.S. armed forces—these three military scholars, at the request of the Pentagon's Office of Net Assessment, undertook this special study of Israel's security revolution. *June 1998, 156 pp., ISBN 0-944029-72-8*

JERUSALEM'S HOLY PLACES AND THE PEACE PROCESS
Marshall J. Breger and Thomas A. Idinopulos

Analyzes more than four hundred years of Jerusalem's history to glean practical, operational lessons from Ottoman, British, Jordanian, and Israeli control of the city and its holy sites: what does and does not work. With the May 1999 deadline for the expiration of the Oslo Accords looming, this study offers a useful guide to shaping a future for Jerusalem based on peace, openness, civility, and tolerance. *Policy Paper no. 46, May 1998, 76 pp., ISBN 0-944029-73-6*

SADAT AND HIS LEGACY
Egypt and the World, 1977–1997
Jon B. Alterman, editor

A far-reaching analysis of the diplomacy and legacy of Anwar Sadat. Based on an international conference commemorating the twentieth anniversary of Sadat's dramatic visit to Jerusalem, this book features presentations by eyewitnesses, scholars, and policymakers. Contributors include Ahmed Maher el-Sayed, Eliahu Ben Elissar, Martin Indyk, Hermann Eilts, Robert Pelletreau, Shibley Telhami, Camelia Sadat and others. With an introduction by Jon B. Alterman and historical appendices featuring Anwar Sadat's and Menachem Begin's addresses to the Knesset in November 1977. *April 1998, 218 pp., ISBN 0-944029-74-4*